Jessica
Merry Christmas 2006
Love From
Aunt Fernie xx xx

BLACK CATS
AND
APRIL FOOLS

BLACK CATS
AND
APRIL FOOLS

BY

HARRY OLIVER

metro

Published by Metro Publishing,
an imprint of John Blake Publishing Ltd,
3 Bramber Court, 2 Bramber Road,
London W14 9PB, England

www.blake.co.uk

First published in hardback in 2006

ISBN-10: 1 84358 162 0
ISBN-13: 978 84358 162 8

British Library Cataloguing-in-Publication Data:

A catalogue record for this book is available from the British Library.

Design by www.envydesign.co.uk

Printed in Great Britain by Creative Print and Design Ltd

1 3 5 7 9 10 8 6 4 2

Papers used by John Blake Publishing are natural, recyclable products
made from wood grown in sustainable forests. The manufacturing
processes conform to the environmental regulations of the
country of origin.

Every attempt has been made to contact the relevant copyright-holders,
but some were unobtainable. We would be grateful if the appropriate
people could contact us.

CONTENTS

Introduction   xi

1   Arts and Entertainment   1

2   Outdoor Dangers   11

3   Actions and Gestures   23

4   Around the Home   33

5   Clothes and Apparel   43

6   Animals   53

7   The Body   81

8   Love and Marriage   97

9   Food and Drink   125

10 Sport and Pastimes   147

11 The Weather and Natural Occurrences   157

12 Birth   173

13 Death   197

14 Numbers, lucky and unlucky   209

15 Gifts   221

16 Celebrations and Festivals   231

17 Days of the Week   247

18 Predicting the Future   255

19 Old Wives' Tales and Pseudo-science   271

20 Flowers and Trees   279

21 International Talismans   291

22 Around the World   301

For Mum, Dad and Claire

ACKNOWLEDGEMENTS

I am thoroughly indebted to my wonderful friends Eleanor Chiari and Gill Partington for their hugely helpful research and advice. Without your assistance things would have been much more difficult!

Mike Mosedale has once again provided superb and amusing illustrations. Thanks Mike, and many thanks also to Graeme Andrew, of Envy Design, who laid out the cover and contents in true style.

Adam Parfitt's editing skills are second to none, and I cannot thank him enough for having taken the time to work on this text.

INTRODUCTION

When I think of old wives' tales and superstitions I think of childhood, which is naturally when I first encountered them, usually as warnings from adults. Whether from parents, grandparents, other people's parents, or even teachers, the authority of whomever told me that walking under a ladder was courting disaster, or that it was unlucky to tread on cracks in the pavement, or that if I broke a mirror it would bring seven years of misfortune, was enough to make me accept this unquestioningly. The need to challenge such 'truths' was peculiarly absent in me: I did not doubt that eating carrots would improve my eyesight, even make me *see in the dark* – I merely assumed that my lack of night vision was down to a deficiency in my consumption of the vegetable! And as for the things I was told would bring me luck – coins in a fountain, seeing a black cat, owning a horseshoe, or finding a four-leaf clover for instance – well what child is going to doubt the logic of something that is going to improve their lot? Not me, anyway. But growing up and developing into a teenager with a defiant streak, combined with the boredom of teenage frustration, meant that the odd transgression such as purposely striding beneath a builder's ladder *just to see what would happen* was irresistible.

And not much did happen, so far as I am aware anyway. But how could I be aware that I didn't deprive myself of a bit of extra luck?! The interesting thing is that all but the most coldly rational of us hold on to superstitions of one sort or another, be they obscure, idiosyncratic notions that many will not have heard of, or more commonly-accepted pieces of received wisdom that we put into practice without even thinking about it. After all, in a society where religion plays an increasingly small part in our lives, 'Bless You' still crops up whenever a sneeze forces its way out of an individual.

The origins of old wives' tales and supersitions are sometimes reasonably obvious, but all too often, they are not! Many are grounded in ancient beliefs, and of course in Christian dogma, but then again a good number have arisen in more recent times. In researching this book, I naturally aimed to provide explanations of the common beliefs we are all aware of, but also wanted to give ample space to the lesser-known, yet still fascinating, ones that may be long gone, or only known of in certain quarters. Many, whose origins remained obscure to me, are listed because they are interesting in themselves, and offer food for thought, and I would be most glad if anyone could fill in any gaps where my research proved fruitless. Do send your thoughts to words@blake.co.uk.

I have tried to create a book for everyone to enjoy, for the superstitious and the cynic alike. On reading it, if you find yourself transformed into a paranoid recluse, wary of leaving the house for fear of the consequences of what may happen to you, then I am sorry. But, 'touch wood', this won't happen, and you will enjoy reading as much as I enjoyed writing. I'll 'keep my fingers crossed' that this is the outcome for most of you! Enjoy!

CHAPTER ONE:
ARTS AND ENTERTAINMENT

'O.K. Frankie...break a leg !'

Break a Leg!

ARTS AND ENTERTAINMENT

Break a leg!

It is considered unlucky to wish an actor 'good luck' before a performance; instead, it is customary to tell him or her to 'break a leg'. The origins and precise meaning of this expression are unclear, and over the years many different experts on superstitions have developed theories as to how it came about. One explanation suggests that, since 'leg' is a euphemism for 'rope' (a taboo word in the theatre as it is on board ships), to tell somebody to 'break a leg' would be equivalent to telling him or her to break the rope holding up the curtain. A particularly good performance, then, would call for the curtain to be open many times in a row for the actor to re-emerge front of the applauding audience, putting it risk of breaking.

Another explanation for the expression link back to Ancient Greece, where audiences stamp their feet instead of clapping their hands at end of a good performance. To tell an actor 'break a leg' would thus not be referring to actor's leg but to that of his or her viewers would have to stamp their feet so much watch their performance. This explanation se unconvincing, however, since the express seems to exist only in English and not in ot Greek-inflected languages.

Eating and drinking food made with lemon milk before a performance

To eat or drink food made with lemon or mil considered very unlucky before a performa The explanation for this superstition is q simple: eating both substances affects sa production, which hinders an actor's voice makes a performance weaker.

Macbeth is the unluckiest of plays

Shakespeare's tragedy *Macbeth* is considered the unluckiest of all plays to put on stage, forecasting disaster for the company performing it and bringing misfortune to those performing in it. The records show that it is the play during which the largest number of accidents, fires and deaths have occurred, and many famous actors who performed the play are said to have had terrible misadventures following its staging. It is considered very unlucky to say the word 'Macbeth' anywhere in the theatre, but especially in the dressing rooms. The play is supposed to be referred to instead as 'that Scottish play', and there are various rituals that actors have to abide by if they accidentally say the 'M' word. According to one tradition, whoever says the forbidden word in the dressing room is to leave the dressing room, turn in a circle three times, break wind or spit and then only come back after knocking and asking permission to re-enter. Another commonly cited remedy is to say 'Angels and ministers of grace defend us!', a line spoken in Act I, sc. iv of *Hamlet* right after the appearance of the Ghost.

The play is generally considered to be unlucky

on account of the appearances of the witches and the occult content of many of the scenes. At the time when Macbeth was first being performed, belief in witchcraft was still widespread and actors may have been afraid of accidentally unleashing demonic forces or conjuring up evil spirits – which is why the line from *Hamlet* would be spoken in protection against any such visitation. Some sources point to a more practical origin for the superstition, however. In Victorian times, theatre managers would close unsuccessful plays and replace them with *Macbeth*, as it was usually a great success due to its violent and bloody scenes and the fact that it could be learned faster than other Shakespeare pieces since it is his shortest tragedy. To hear the word 'Macbeth' spoken in the dressing room would thus be an omen of very bad luck for actors who risked finding themselves out of work very soon. It is also possible that the bad statistics for the performance of the play may be explained precisely because it was used so often as a replacement and filler in theatre seasons.

Whistling during a performance brings bad luck
It is considered very unlucky to whistle anywhere

near the stage during a performance as this is supposed to curse it and bring doom upon it. One simple explanation for this is that theatre technicians would sometimes be given the signal to raise a prop or send down a backdrop using some form of whistling code. Whistling backstage could inadvertently send the wrong signal and seriously ruin a play.

To see the ghost of Drury Lane

It is a stroke of good fortune for an actor to see the ghost of Drury Lane before a performance as it announces a long and brilliant career. The ghost, known as 'the man in grey' (because of the long grey overcoat it is seen wearing), apparently haunts the Theatre Royal on Drury Lane, in London. The ghost is usually seen in the daytime in the auditorium of the theatre, the oldest in London after the reconstructed Globe Theatre. The man in grey also wears a powdered wig, a tricorne hat and carries a sword. Some say the apparition is the ghost of a man murdered in the theatre whose skeleton was found in 1840 in a walled-in room backstage, with a dagger stuck in its ribcage.

There are many other ghost stories surrounding theatres, and Monday night was traditionally considered 'ghost night', a time when ghosts were thought to come out to perform their own plays. Apparently, this old belief lies behind the practice, still common today, of not having performances on Monday. The term 'ghost light' is also linked to superstitious beliefs about ghosts. Besides helping people find their bearings backstage and avoiding terrible accidents, this kind of backstage lighting that was originally provided by candles was there to scare off the ghosts of past performances thought to haunt the stage and interfere with existing performances.

Never speak a play's last line during rehearsals
In acting circles it is considered very unlucky to say the last line of a play out loud before the night of the performance, as it tempts fate and may expose the play to evil forces. The play, in fact, is not considered 'finished' until it is performed. This superstition resembles the superstition warning a bride against wearing the completed wedding gown before her wedding day, and may be a form of protection against evil

spirits or the Devil – they cannot start attacking the wedding or the performance until it is officially 'ready' and under way.

Wearing green, yellow or blue at the theatre
These colours are believed to be unlucky when worn at the theatre. The bad luck associated with wearing the colour blue is apparently neutralised if silver is worn with it. The explanation for this superstition lies in the cost of producing blue textiles during the early days of theatre. Back in a time before synthetic dyes were common, the dye that was used to produce blue cloth was extremely expensive: if a company used blue costumes they could be assumed to be going over budget and endangering their finances. If silver was added to the costume, however, this was a clear sign that the theatre company had a very wealthy patron.

The superstitions around wearing green and yellow at the theatre have various interpretations. Some sources say that during Elizabethan times yellow and green were considered the colours of the Devil due to the destructive forces of fire and the savage forces of the forest. These same sources point out that green was also the colour of the fairies and thus a dangerous colour to wear. In fact, there is little evidence of any dislike of the colour green in Elizabethan plays and other texts, and it doesn't seem to be deemed unlucky until the seventeenth century. Other sources have argued more pragmatically that green and yellow were considered unlucky at the theatre because the lighting that used to be common in the past would make those colours virtually invisible on stage and thus an actor's performance would be hindered by his or her near invisibility.

CHAPTER 2

OUTDOOR DANGERS

'Stone me!... if that isn't the third one today '

It is unlucky to walk under a ladder

OUTDOOR DANGERS

Walking under a ladder

This is one of the most commonly held superstitions, still believed by many people who do not think themselves superstitious. It is considered very unfortunate to walk under a ladder, but there are various interpretations of what is meant to befall those who ignore the custom. Most people believe it will simply bring bad luck, a belief grounded in the possibility of objects or paint falling on the reckless pedestrian from workers on the ladder or above it. Some people believe that distracted passers-by who walk under a ladder could be sure not to get married on the year of the transgression, while other versions of the superstition predicted the gallows for the unlucky walker. The most cited origination of this superstition, however, is that the ladder is seen to form a triangle with the wall and the ground, a triangle suggesting the Holy Trinity: to walk through that triangle would be to call misfortune upon oneself by showing disrespect to the Trinity.

Other recent sources point instead to the negative symbolism of ladders in general, such as the ladder that was used to take Jesus off the cross, or the ladder used to lead inmates to the gallows (this last explanation supporting the idea that walking under a ladder is an omen pointing to a date with the hangman – not something most of us need worry about nowadays!).

Finding money

Oddly, you may think, it was once considered very unlucky to find money on the ground. This belief dates as far back as the sixteenth century. In order to help ensure that they did not have to deal with the misfortune that would result from discovering a few handy coppers lying around, wily individuals took protective measures, the most common being to spit on the found money. If the coins were somehow damaged, they were considered lucky and could be picked up without any danger. The origins of this superstition are unclear but one could imagine that a poor person found in possession of coins might be accused of theft, and a broken or damaged coin would most likely have been discarded by its owner and would thus pose no threat to those who found it. It may also be that the superstition was spread as a general protective measure for the good of the community, to make it more likely that lost money would be returned to its original owner. Nowadays, it would surely take a truly superstitious individual to walk past a few coins glinting at them in the sun ...

Stepping on a crack in the pavement
It is considered unlucky to step on cracks in the pavement. Today this belief is often held by children who know the rhyme 'Step on a crack, break your mother's back' (assuming they're not in a sulk with their mothers, that is). This superstition dates back to the late nineteenth century, when a racist version of today's rhyme

became popular. Although the supposed logic behind it is unclear, the original rhyme suggested that, were one to step on the cracks, one would have a black baby, which during that racist time was considered an unlucky event. A later version of the rhyme turned into 'Step on a crack and your mother will turn black', which then shifted again, probably sometime in the 1950s, to its non-racist modern equivalent. Another superstition surrounding stepping on cracks linked the number of cracks one stepped on and the number of dishes you would break that day, though the origins of this version of the superstition are difficult to ascertain.

Parting at bridges, crossing bridges and walking under them

Bridges, because they are often suspended between two stretches of land or over the dangers of water, have evoked several popular superstitions. Perhaps the most common is the belief that if one says goodbye to a friend on a bridge this is a sure sign that you will never see that person again: the bridge is a symbol of separation, with each friend belonging to a different stretch of land and growing apart. There are several superstitions warning against being the first person to cross a new bridge because the Devil, called to the bridge by his envy at man's ability to build something so complex, would avenge himself by taking the soul of the first person to cross it. Sometimes animals would be sent across the bridge first as a preventive measure against such an occurrence. In Norway it was once thought that trolls lived under bridges, so it was important to have something to give them or flatter them with so they would not pester those who wanted to cross (and this myth has reached English culture in the form of the story of the Three Billy Goats Gruff). It is common for those who work on constructing bridges to leave a symbolic amount of money in the plaster or cement making up the bridge to protect it and bring it good luck in the years to come. Wine is also sometimes used for the same purpose: bottles of wine are broken against the surface of the bridge when it is opened in the same way that is done for baptising ships. In some places it is considered very unlucky to walk under a bridge while a train or other vehicle is passing above, for the perhaps obvious reason that the bridge may collapse under such weight. To counter such a superstition, people are supposed to touch the roof of their car if they are driving, or spit, or cross their fingers. Touching the roof of the car is clearly a gesture intended to hold the bridge up. But please, should you feel the need to do this while driving, only use one hand – letting go of the steering wheel altogether seems far more likely to bring disaster to the modern driver.

Crossroads

In the past, crossroads were considered very dangerous places where one was likely to meet spirits, in particular the ghosts of suicides (who would often be buried there so that their soul would be confused and would not know how to find its way back to the place where it died). Crossroads marked the border between the safe world of the village and the home, and the unknown where magic, danger and adventure began. It was also common to place hanging gallows at large intersections just outside cities and villages, so crossroads were unpleasant and frightening places to walk past. When it wasn't their dead bodies left hanging and rotting for all to see, the ghosts of those who had been executed could possibly also be haunting these places. In Catholic countries, small altars to local saints or to the Virgin Mary are often found at crossroads in back streets out in the countryside, perhaps the last remnant of an archaic search for protection. In ancient times sacrifices would sometimes take place at crossroads. In Scandinavia, trolls were thought to gather at crossroads, while in the British Isles it was witches and fairies, and in India and Ancient Greece crossroads marked openings to the world of the gods and the dead.

Precautions for travellers, or advice for a happy holiday

In the past, travelling could be a very frightening and dangerous activity, so it is not surprising that many superstitions evolved around the act of setting out on a journey. A traveller leaving their home would look up at the sky and at the landscape around to notice any movement of wildlife. Anything appearing on the left side of the traveller was considered a bad omen for the journey, while anything appearing on the right

19

was considered auspicious. To return home after setting off, for whatever reason, was considered very unlucky and likely to curse the entire trip. It was recommended, if returning home was unavoidable, that the traveller leave again the following morning, or that they perform various purification rituals before setting out again, such as lighting a candle in the local church or spitting and making the sign of the cross. It was considered bad luck to look back towards home having left, and it was also considered unlucky for those left behind to watch the traveller until they disappeared behind the horizon.

A superstition that many people still believe in today relates to St Christopher, the patron saint of travellers: to wear a silver medal or to carry around a small statue of the saint is said to protect the traveller from any misfortune. This superstition is clearly based in the Catholic tradition, where patron saints are believed to protect all aspects of daily life. The name Christopher comes from the Greek *kristos* (Christ) and *phero* (to carry) and is connected to a myth about a giant to whom the baby Christ appeared in the form of a small child wanting to cross a river. The giant carried the child across. The amulets of St Christopher always depict a tall man carrying a stick and a small baby on his back or in his arms. So next time you have a holiday from hell, perhaps you shouldn't just blame the holiday rep or the monstrous building site blocking your sea-view – think about how you may be partly to blame for not having paid heed to this wealth of superstitions. Or just stop going on those package deals ...

Having a woman on board a ship

In the past it was considered very unlucky to have a woman on a ship, especially a prostitute, as it was thought that her presence would cause storms and possibly shipwreck. This superstition probably originated from the social tensions and problems that might arise among the crew of bachelor men if a woman was on board, and from the sense that sex would distract sailors from their duties aboard the ship. An extension of this superstition led to the practice of having scantily clad or completely naked women carved on the bow of ships, as offerings to the seas who were thought to be calmed by the sight of female nudity. These days, with some women single-

21

handedly sailing yachts around the globe, it seems that having a woman on board a ship can actually lead to great things.

CHAPTER THREE:
ACTIONS AND GESTURES

'Lottery win or not...that's just plain rude !'

It is rude to point...

ACTIONS AND GESTURES

Never light three cigarettes with the same match
It is considered very unlucky to light three cigarettes with the same match, and it is especially taboo in military circles. This superstition harks back to the Boer War, although it is more often associated with the long nights in the trenches of the First World War. Snipers from enemy lines would notice the match being struck to light the first cigarette; they had time to load their gun as the second cigarette was being lit; and they could confidently aim and fire at the unlucky third smoker as the burning match reached his

cigarette. Remember this the next time you find yourself in a battle situation and the nicotine cravings kick in.

Crossing fingers

To cross one's fingers is a gesture used to ward off evil and bring good luck. It is thought to be an attempt at conjuring up the protection of the Christian cross and Jesus Christ. It is considered unlucky, however, to arrange objects (especially silverware) in the shape of the cross, as this is seen as an offence against God. Fingers are thus crossed on the same hand forming a slanted cross, rather than across hands in true cross shape. Crossing fingers is also a gesture used as a countermeasure when one has accidentally walked under a ladder, and it is commonly used by children when telling a lie as a way of protecting themselves in advance for the consequences of the bad deed. There is little evidence of people crossing fingers as a sign of good luck before the late nineteenth century. In the past it was much more common to cross one's legs or to wrap one's thumb with the other fingers of the hand. The practice of folding thumbs inside one's hands is still used in Switzerland in the same way crossing fingers is used in the British Isles, Ireland and North America.

Touching wood

Touching wood is a gesture (or simply an invocation when the expression 'touch wood' is spoken) used to counter the threat one may incur when boasting or willing something to happen – or not to happen. Today simply saying 'touch wood' is considered enough, but in the past it was always necessary actually to touch wood. The practice of touching wood may be an inheritance from the ancient understanding that speaking of one's good fortune would anger the gods and tempt fate. The practice is often associated with seeking the protection of the wood of the cross, or with ancient beliefs in benevolent wood gods and spirits that could be conjured up for protection by a knock or a touch. Other sources, however, argue that the custom of touching wood is not ancient at all and is simply derived from a nineteenth-century children's game called 'tig-touch-wood', in which children would be 'safe' during a game of tag when they were touching wood. All of the explanations have their merits, but which is the definitive origin is uncertain. Americans, incidentally, say 'knock on wood' rather than 'touch wood'.

Throwing a shoe for luck

It was customary, from as far back as the sixteenth century, to throw an old shoe after a person departing (on foot, by carriage or by ship) for good luck. The custom was extended to cars, and remains today only in the disappearing practice of tying an old pair of shoes to the back of newlyweds' cars. The shoes are meant to bring good luck and fertility to the couple. The origins of this superstition are unknown and puzzling. It may be that since shoes were precious goods in the past, to throw one behind a person would suggest abundance and wealth, throwing the shoe being something equivalent to throwing a coin into a fountain, constituting a sacrifice of sorts. Another possible explanation might relate to the journey: since the shoe being thrown is old, the gesture may bring good luck in the sense of suggesting that the person departing might return with a new shoe (or hopefully a pair) for the loved one left behind.

Pointing a finger brings bad luck

In the past, to point a finger at somebody was considered very unlucky. To point at somebody was seen as equivalent to cursing them because it was thought that the index finger would concentrate evil forces in the direction it was pointed; it would also bring misfortune to the person pointing the finger by causing anger and conflict. It was considered particularly unlucky to point at a funeral procession as this gesture was bound to bring a new death in the town. Similarly, it was thought to be unlucky to point at rainbows, stars or the moon – these gestures, in fact, were seen as sinful and disrespectful (this belief may be a remnant from ancient times when these natural phenomena were worshipped). At times of heightened hysteria about witchcraft, women were arrested simply for pointing their finger in the direction of someone. Today the action of pointing a finger and the expression 'to point a finger at someone' are both read as gestures of accusation and we no longer see it as a gesture that brings bad luck. It is likely, however, that the idea that it is rude and inappropriate derived from this old superstition.

Throwing coins into a fountain for luck

It is considered good luck to throw coins into a fountain. The origins of this gesture are ancient, dating back to a time when all bodies of water were thought to be inhabited by gods, spirits or fairies. Originally it was customary to throw pieces of a sacrificed body into the water (only very early on would these sacrifices have been of human bodies – they soon consisted rather of animal sacrifices, or even statues and figurines made out of wood, stone or bone) in order to appease the water spirit. Today the gesture is thought to bring good luck in the form of a wish come true. If one makes a wish, it is normally customary to throw the coin over one's shoulder, tossing it backwards into the fountain or well. In Rome, when one throws a coin into the famous Trevi Fountain, visitors are recommended one day to wish to return to Rome. So when in Rome ...

Making the sign of the cross

To make the sign of the cross was thought to bring luck and protection from misfortune and was often used as a gesture against evil forces. Today it is common for sportsmen to cross themselves before attempting a particularly challenging sports feat, or for gamblers to sit cross-legged in the hope of having luck on their side. In the past, the sign of the cross was more commonly seen, for example, written on bread before being put in the oven or marked on doors and cribs to protect from evil witches. The sign of the cross was also thought to bring healing from very early in history, as far back as AD 1000. The gesture is a general symbol of blessing bestowed upon the congregation during Catholic ceremonies. It is still common for people to cross themselves upon seeing a funeral procession so as to bless the deceased and those dear to him or her and to ensure protection from any ill will coming from the dead. There is also the familiar childhood saying 'crossing my heart', often followed by 'and hope to die', when making a promise, calling the power of the cross against oneself if the promise is broken. The origins of this expression are obscure but its use seems confined to the world of child play, probably only dating back to the nineteenth century.

CHAPTER FOUR:
AROUND THE HOME

RUGBY CLUB

'Look mate...that umbrella is one action
too far in this environment.'

It is unlucky to open an umbrella indoors.

AROUND THE HOME

Breaking a mirror

To break a mirror is said to bring seven years of bad luck. If a mirror breaks of its own accord, this is also considered a terrible omen, foretelling the death of someone dear to the mirror's owner. The origins of this superstition may be linked to ancient beliefs surrounding reflections more generally, which were seen to have magical properties and to retain something of the soul of the person looking into them. To shatter a reflection by creating ripples in water or by breaking a mirror would thus be seen as dangerous for the soul, exposing it to witchcraft, to the working of the Devil or of evil spirits. The reasons for the bad luck being for seven years may be linked to the connection between the number seven and the fact that God created the world in seven days. There would thus be a cycle of bad or good fortune spanning seven years in parallel to the seven days of God's creation. The superstition may, however, also be linked to the even more ancient notion that the most important changes in life occur over seven-year time periods. The damaging influence of the broken mirror would thus affect people for the entire duration of a seven-year cycle unless countermeasures were taken. The two best-known remedies for the broken mirror curse are throwing the broken pieces of the mirror into a river, or burying them in sacred ground.

Hanging a horseshoe over a threshold

Horseshoes are among the most celebrated symbols of good luck and they are constantly represented in cards, wedding confetti and charm bracelets. Their main purpose is to ward off evil, although finding a horseshoe or walking under a threshold over which an iron horseshoe has been hanged are both thought to be particularly lucky events. The origins of this superstition are unclear. Some associate the power of the horseshoe to the fact that it is made of iron, a metal considered powerful since ancient times, and made even more powerful by its Christian association with the nails of the cross. In the British Isles it was common to think that fairies and witches did not like iron and stood clear of it. Others associate the horseshoe to early horse-worshipping rituals or link the crescent shape of the horseshoe to the moon or rainbows, which were both considered lucky symbols and were worshipped in pre-Christian societies. Horseshoes with seven holes in them are traditionally the luckiest of all, given the number seven's association with the supernatural. There is much debate over which is the best way to hang a horseshoe over a doorway. Most people believe it should be arranged pointing upwards to ensure that good fortune does not slip away; but others hold the opposite view and say that a downward positioning of the horseshoe ensures that the good fortune will be transmitted to those walking beneath it.

Placing objects on the table

Perhaps because the table is symbolic of the church's altar within the household, there are many taboos about objects being placed on the table. A more practical reason could be simply connected with issues of hygiene and protection from germs, an interpretation that would also explain why these superstitions can only be traced back to the mid-nineteenth century. It was then, in fact, that even ordinary people were becoming aware of the existence of germs and their dangerous workings within the household. Placing one's shoes on the table is considered very unlucky. Babies, bellows, umbrellas and lanterns are also forbidden items. There is also a superstition associated with sitting on the table: if you do so you will never get married. If a guest folds his napkin at the end of a meal this is supposed to be a sign that they will never return to that household, so take note of this at your next dinner party and, if you're keen to hold on to your friends, just don't provide napkins.

Opening an umbrella indoors

The belief that opening an umbrella indoors

brings bad luck is widespread to this day. Its origins cannot be traced back much earlier than the late nineteenth century, since umbrellas have only been in common use in Europe since the beginning of that century. The superstition has nevertheless undergone some transformation. In earlier versions it was thought to be an omen of death. The most likely explanation for the superstition is connected to the taboo concerning gestures and actions meant for one environment being made in another, so that actions meant for the outdoors must not be performed indoors.

Getting up 'on the wrong side of the bed'

Implying that somebody is in a bad mood or generally unfortunate, this phrase has its roots in popular superstition. The 'right' side of the bed was normally thought to be the opposite side from the one the bed was entered into the night before. This idea that things should be done in opposites is true of many other superstitions, as for example in the importance attributed to transporting a corpse out of the house feet first – the opposite to one's position at the time of birth. These gestures were thought to 'open' and 'close' an event properly, so to get off on the same side of the bed as one entered into it would be to expose oneself to evil spirits for not having given proper closure to the ritual of sleep. In later years it became common always to consider the right as the correct side to get out of bed from, since it represented the side of good, the left being traditionally associated with the Devil (see the entry on left and right hands on page 90). In these times of singledom and limited living space in cities, many of us have our beds up against the walls, so there is a good chance that many always get up on the wrong side of the bed!

Turning a calendar page before the new month has started

It is considered very bad luck to turn the page in a calendar before the arrival of the month depicted on the page. This superstition appears to be fairly recent, dating back no later than the early twentieth century when mass-produced paper calendars became widespread. The reason for the superstition, however, is based in the ancient fear of tempting fate. In this case the temptation would come from assuming that one

will be alive and well in the future, something
only God (or the gods) was to decide.

Dropping silverware

To drop silverware on the floor was thought to be
a sign that a visit was imminent. This superstition
dates back to the early nineteenth century and its
origins are unclear. If one dropped a knife then
the visitor would be a man; if one dropped a fork
the visitor would be a woman; and if one dropped
a spoon it would be a child. Sometimes to drop a
spoon would therefore also be a sign of an
imminent pregnancy. The reasons for the
different genders being associated with the
silverware illustrate the gender stereotypes that
often characterise popular superstitions, the knife
being a more aggressive implement than a fork.
Spoons were often smaller in size than knives and
forks and that was probably the reason they were
thought to refer to children. When they were
connected to pregnancy this may have been due
to their rounded shape, not unlike a woman's in
the later months of the pregnancy.

Hanging seaweed on the mantelpiece

In the past it was thought that hanging seaweed above the mantelpiece would protect the house from fires. This belief can only be seen to date back to the middle of the nineteenth century. Its origins can probably be explained by the simple association of seaweed with water and to the idea that, since water is fire's natural opposite, seaweed would be a good talisman against fire.

Making sure there is always something in the oven

An old Jewish superstition says that leaving an oven empty will cause the family to go hungry in the future. To prevent such a misfortune from befalling a household, however, it is enough to leave a baking sheet or a pan in the oven as a precaution. This superstition may be linked to very ancient rituals in which food was always left for household gods in order to ensure their protection of the family. In Rome, household gods had altars of their own and were given small portions of food to appease them.

CHAPTER FIVE:
CLOTHES AND APPAREL

'The kids love it...but I'm afraid
I'd set my heart on a left fitting shoe.'

CLOTHES AND APPAREL

Buttons

It is thought that doing up the buttons of one's shirt incorrectly is a clear sign of bad luck. The recommended cure is quite simple though: to take off the garment and start again! To find a button in the street is supposed to be a good omen, foretelling the beginning of a new friendship, and buttons with four holes in them are considered particularly lucky. It is also considered good luck to give buttons as a gift. These traditions only date back to the nineteenth century, though in the late seventeenth century diviners used buttons to predict the future, asking them questions and picking up a handful at random. Whether they picked up an even or odd number would determine whether the answer was a 'yes' or a 'no'. Buttons have thus been attributed magic properties for longer than the superstitions surrounding found buttons have been around. The tradition of using buttons for divination has remained in certain children's rhymes sung when counting buttons: 'This year, next year, now, never' and 'Tinker, tailor, soldier, sailor, rich man, poor man, beggar man, thief'. When children recited these rhymes counting buttons, the word the last button was counted on would stand for a person's destiny or the destiny of their future husband. The rhyme 'This year, next year, now, never' was usually thought to answer the question of whether and when a person would marry.

Shoes

Perhaps because shoes were extremely expensive items in the past, or because they were made to suit their owners (and could thus seem to be extensions of their bodies), there are many superstitions associated with them. It is considered bad luck accidentally to put shoes on the wrong feet. This superstition dates back to Roman times when the

Emperor Augustus only narrowly escaped an assassination attempt after putting his sandals on backwards. If shoelaces continuously come untied it is supposed to be a sign of good news coming your way, perhaps in the form of a letter. It is bad luck to place shoes on a table (see the entry concerning objects on the table on page 38), and shoes placed on a bed are supposed to be omens of an imminent death in the family. In the past people used to say that, if you didn't give a new pair of shoes to a poor man in your lifetime, then you would go barefoot in the afterlife. The origins of this superstition can be guessed to be incentives for people to help the poor. In some areas of England and northern Europe, it was once thought that turning one's shoes with the buckles and laces closest to the bed would help prevent nightmares. This belief was probably linked to the idea that witches and fairies didn't like knots or metal and, since Anglo-Saxons and Norsemen believed that nightmares were brought about by a *mara*, an evil fairy-demon creature that would ride on the chest of sleepers at night, holding them by the hair, having the knots and metal bolts of shoes next to the sleeper's bed were probably reasonable precautions.

New clothes at Easter

Wearing new clothes at Easter is a tradition that also contains a bit of superstition in it. It was thought that failing to wear at least one new item of clothing on Easter Sunday would bring bad luck. This belief has both a practical and a symbolic origin to it. The practical origin is connected to the fact that in many places people observed Lent by wearing the same outfit during the entire forty days (or at least it was considered sinful to buy new clothes during that period). The symbolic reason is that Easter is a time of regeneration for the Earth after the death of Christ: as a time of renewal it was the ideal moment to purchase a new outfit, for the poor perhaps the only outfit they would own until the next year.

Aprons

If a woman's apron comes untied, this is a sign that her sweetheart is thinking about her. Other versions of the superstition simply state that 'somebody' is thinking about her. This superstition only dates back to the early nineteenth century, and its origins are unclear, although there are two possible explanations. The first is simply connected to the slightly sexual idea of untying a woman's apron, perhaps something the presumed lover would like to do; the second, which is less modern, is connected to the idea that knots in clothing were used against witches and spells. That a knot comes untied of its own accord suggests that a spell has been cast on the woman, removing her 'defences' – though she may not be that eager to keep up such defences in the first place.

Gloves

It is considered unlucky for a person to pick up his or her own glove if it falls to the ground. One should wait for a friend to pick it up instead. When the glove is returned, it is recommended not to say 'thank you', as a final precaution against bad luck. Some sources assume that this superstition originated in medieval times when ladies used to make the gesture of dropping gloves for their knights to pick up as a sign of romantic interest. There seems to be little evidence for this connection in written records, and the superstition only begins to appear in accounts dating back to the early twentieth century. To drop a glove in medieval times was actually a gesture of defiance and challenge, anticipating a duel if the challenged person chose to pick up the glove. Perhaps having a friend pick up the glove and return it is a way of neutralising the bad feeling that could come from a 'challenge'. Much like the superstition surrounding scissors and knives, which requires a person to pay a symbolic amount for those sharp objects (see page 223), friends who are given a pair of gloves as a present are supposed to pay the donor a symbolic sum to prevent any bad feelings from harming the friendship. It is supposed to be unlucky to lose a pair of gloves, not only because one's hands will consequently be cold, but also supposedly because the gloves could fall into the hands of witches. It is, instead, considered very lucky to find gloves in the street, especially on Sundays when such an occurrence is an omen of a great week to come.

Hats

It is considered extremely unlucky to put a hat on a bed or on a table. A hat on a bed announces a death to come. This superstition may have come from a time when doctors paid home visits to patients. If a patient was very seriously ill, the doctor would be rushing to his or her bedside and would not have had time to take his hat off upon entering the house, which was the normal polite thing to do. He would more likely take the hat off at the patient's bedside, perhaps only once he became aware that there was nothing left to do for his patient. A hat on the table is unlucky for the same reasons that shoes on the table are unlucky: a combination of hygienic concerns and fear of being disrespectful since the table is like an altar within the home. Another superstition surrounding hats, which has now fallen out of use, concerns their use in church for women. It was considered very unlucky for a woman to take her hat off in church. This probably stemmed from the belief that a woman's hair would tempt men attending the service to be distracted by desire and lose sight of the holy thoughts and words they aimed to encounter during the service.

Underwear

A strange superstition says that if a person is having a bad day they can make the day better by turning their underwear inside out. The origins of this superstition are unknown and puzzling and, although some men in the throes of bachelorhood have been reported to turn their used boxer shorts inside out before stepping back into them, it seems this is motivated by laziness and lack of alternative underwear rather than a desire for a change in fortune! If a single woman borrows underwear from a married woman, this is supposed to ensure she will get married within the year.

CHAPTER SIX:
ANIMALS

'I'm sorry m'lud...the defendent was crushed
by a motorist on the way to court.'

Hedgehogs steal cows' milk!

ANIMALS

Black cats are lucky

The belief that black cats are lucky is relatively recent, dating only from the mid-1800s. Older records from the seventeenth century show that they were more likely to be considered unlucky, but also that the precise significance of a black cat depended on the circumstances in which it is encountered. To see it walking towards you is a good omen, for instance, but if it crosses your path it is a harbinger of evil, especially in the morning. Those in dangerous professions, such as miners and fishermen, would often turn back and refuse to go to work that day if a black cat ran in front of them. This fear of a black cat crossing one's path persists today in the USA and certain other parts of the world, and in some places spitting is said to be the only way to avert the bad luck it brings.

Whether lucky or unlucky, the black cat has long been seen as having special powers. Bast, the black female cat goddess, was worshipped in Ancient Egypt, and in Europe the black cat is traditionally linked to witchcraft. The black cat as a witch's familiar is an image common in folklore and storybooks, and records show that it was often believed to be the witch herself, in animal form. This association with magic and the supernatural perhaps explains why in the past it was considered to have the power to cure ailments. Folk remedies from the seventeenth century often feature a black cat: rubbing its tail into the eye was a traditional cure for a stye, and drinking its blood was believed to restore health. Other gruesome recipes include gravy made from stewed black cat as a cure for consumption, and a cat's head, burned and powdered, as a remedy for failing eyesight.

Cats have nine lives

According to this familiar old wives' tale, cats have an unusual ability to escape death, and may 'die' nine times yet still survive. This idea dates back to at least the sixteenth century and, although its precise source is unclear, it probably has its origins in the traditional link between cats and the supernatural. The Ancient Egyptians, who venerated cats as gods, viewed them as immortal. More recently, cats have been associated with witchcraft, and it was said that a witch could take on the body of a cat nine times. This fear of cats as demonic creatures is reflected in the old tradition of entering a house with the greeting 'God bless all except the cat'.

A cat should not be left alone with a corpse

When a dead family member was laid out in the house prior to the funeral, cats were kept well away to prevent them jumping on to or over the body. Should this happen, the cat must be immediately killed or dire consequences would ensue: either the spirit of the dead person would be endangered, or else the next person to see the body would die. Accordingly, cats were often trapped under an overturned tub until the funeral was safely over. The precise origin of this belief is unclear, but once again it seems to be related to the idea that cats are supernatural or even demonic creatures.

There are other related superstitions linking cats with death: a cat can supposedly foretell a death and will refuse to stay indoors if a member of the family is about to die. They are also reputed to have the ability to 'suck the breath' out of infants, and therefore must never be left alone with one. Records show that this belief was so widespread that, in the eighteenth century, one coroner actually found a cat responsible for the death of a child!

Transferring disease to a cat or dog
According to superstition, human illness can be cured by transferring it to a cat or dog. The origin of this idea is not certain, but it has been in existence since at least the eighteenth century, when a recommended cure for a sore hand was to place a finger in a cat's ear until the sufferer's affliction was gone, only to reappear in the cat. In the Victorian period, parents would attempt to

cure a sick child by placing a lock of its hair in a dog's food. Reputedly, the illness would move mysteriously from the child to the animal, whereupon the former would recover at the expense of the latter.

One for sorrow, two for joy ...
Magpies are heavily associated with superstitious beliefs, but their precise significance varies according to their number, as is well known from the popular rhyme:

One for sorrow
Two for joy
Three for a girl
Four for a boy
Five for silver
Six for gold
Seven for a secret never to be told

The verse exists in many different variations, and it seems to date back at least to the eighteenth century, when the following version is recorded in Lincolnshire:

One for sorrow,
Two for mirth,
Three for a wedding,
And four for death.

Before this point, however, superstitions are less concerned with numbers of magpies than with their behaviour. Like many birds, they are regarded as messengers, telling of things to come. To see one sitting noisily in a tree foretold the arrival of a stranger, whereas, if a magpie were to sit on a roof or fly repeatedly around a house making its chattering sound, it meant the imminent death of a family member. Seen on the way to church, a magpie was again a death omen. A bird capable of foretelling such misfortune had to be treated with caution, and at one time it was common to remove one's hat and bow on encountering a magpie. Alternatively, people made the sign of the cross on meeting one, saying,

I cross the magpie,
The magpie crosses me;
Bad luck to the magpie,
And good luck to me.

The magpie's sinister reputation can be traced back
to the Old Testament: it was the only creature that
refused to enter Noah's Ark, but instead sat on the
roof. With its distinctive black and white plumage,
it is said to be the illicit offspring of the dove and
the raven, and was not therefore baptised along
with God's other creatures.

The first cuckoo of spring
Hearing the first cuckoo of spring is said to be of
great importance, since the circumstances may
reveal the hearer's future. To hear it from the left
is unlucky, whereas on the right it denotes luck for
the year to come. Those looking down at the
ground on hearing it will be dead within the next
twelve months. Another old wives' tale states that
what someone is doing when they first hear the
cuckoo sets the pattern for the year ahead.
Accordingly, it is considered lucky to be carrying
money at the time since this indicates a year of
prosperity. Turning over the coins in your pocket
brings especially good fortune at this moment,
and it was common for someone who had no
coins quickly to borrow one for this purpose. It
was also well known for people to break into a run

on hearing the first cuckoo, so as to avoid being idle in the forthcoming year. For similar reasons it is supposed to be bad luck to hear the cuckoo while lying in bed, since this indicates a year of illness or laziness, although possibly this tale was designed to encourage those reluctant to get out of bed.

The length of the cuckoo's song is also important. In the nineteenth century, a children's rhyme asked,

Cuckoo, cherry tree,
Good bird, tell me,
How many years I shall be,
Before I die?

The number of notes sounded by the bird then indicated the number of years until death. A similar rhyme was also used to tell how many years before marriage. A more unusual marriage superstition, dating from the seventeenth century, dictated that, on hearing the first cuckoo, the hearer should take off their right shoe, and would find a strand of hair. Its colour would be that of their future spouse. It is not difficult to see why superstitions, especially marriage superstitions, are attached to the cuckoo, since its distinctive call is one of the first signs of the arrival of the season associated with fertility and growth.

Telling the bees

According to the old wives' tale, bees must be told about any important family event, especially a wedding or death, otherwise they may either fly away or die. It was even common to involve the bees in such events, bringing them a piece of wedding cake or draping their hives in black for a funeral. References to the practice of telling the bees are found in Ancient Greece, but it became especially common in the nineteenth century, when they would be informed of a death by gently tapping the hive and reciting the phrase 'Little brownie, little brownie, your master's dead'. If, after a few moments, the bees began to hum once more, they showed their intent to remain in the hive. Often the beehives would be symbolically turned around on the occasion of a burial. This was not without its risks, however. A funeral procession in Devon was left in disarray when the horses bolted and took the coffin with them after being attacked by angry bees. A hapless servant had misunderstood his instructions and overturned the hives!

A number of other superstitions involve bees. They should never be bought or sold for money, for instance, but instead bartered with goods. A bee flying into a house means the imminent arrival of a stranger. Most peculiar of all, a virgin may walk through a swarm of bees without being stung. In most such superstitions, bees seem to be wise and benevolent. This may be because they are said to have originated in heaven and were God's 'little servants'.

Bats seen in daylight
The appearance of bats in daylight is generally considered to be an ill omen, and superstitions dating from the seventeenth century warn that a bat flying into a house is a harbinger of death or disaster. This is probably because bats, as a creature of the night, have been associated with witchcraft and black magic. They are even thought to have the power to bewitch a person if allowed close enough.

However, charms made out of bat bones and

eyes are thought to bring good luck and, as long ago as the first century AD, the Roman writer Pliny recommended nailing a bat upside-down above a door in order to repel bad fortune.

Killing a robin brings bad luck

The belief that harming a robin is bad luck goes back to the eighteenth century. Killing one reputedly brought a lifetime of bad fortune, and breaking its leg would result in the same injury to the culprit. Children fond of collecting birds' eggs would be sure not to interfere with the nest of a robin for fear their fingers would grow crooked. The superstition seems to come from the idea that the robin is a sacred bird, enjoying divine protection. An old saying states that

Little Cock Robin and Little Jenny Wren,
Are God Almighty's Little Cock and Hen.

However, in the nineteenth century, it is just as common to find examples of robins feared as a harbinger of death. A robin is believed to tap three times at the window of the room in which a person is about to shuffle off this mortal coil, and, should one be seen perching on the top of a house while singing its plaintive song, it is a sure sign that a baby in the house will die.

Beware of large black dogs

The ghostly figure of a large black dog is said to haunt murder sites or other places of death. Spine-chilling tales have been told since at least the seventeenth century of the sinister black dog, or 'Barghest', who is said to have large red eyes, or is sometimes described as headless. The story goes that this is no ordinary dog, but the Devil in disguise.

Owls are a bad omen

Seeing or hearing an owl, especially in daylight, is considered to portend death or some other calamity. This old wives' tale is very old indeed, being found in Ancient Rome and throughout the Middle Ages in England. Both Chaucer and Shakespeare mention the owl as an omen of death, and in the eighteenth century a commentator warns that 'if an Owl ... sends forth its hoarse and dismal Voice, it is an Omen of the Approach of some terrible Thing; that some dire

Calamity ... is near at Hand'. The reasons for this are unclear, but in some cultures owls are seen as gods of the underworld, and in Germany it is known as a witch's bird. Those who have heard the unearthly screech of an owl will not be surprised that it is viewed with fear.

A less sinister belief states that an owl heard hooting near houses indicates that someone is about to lose their virginity.

Stepping on a beetle brings rain

Those who wish for dry weather should avoid standing on a black beetle, as this is reputed to bring wet weather, according to an old wives' tale from the Victorian period. Picking it up and burying it is sometimes supposed to counteract this, however.

Sacrificing a calf cures the herd

If a herd of cows is struck down with illness, a gruesome custom dictated that the farmer should either burn or bury alive his best calf. The rest of the herd, having walked over its grave, would be cured. A related superstition states that a spate of miscarriages in cattle would be cured by hanging the body of one of the premature calves, hooves uppermost, in a tree close to the herd. Alternatively, its severed leg was hung up either in the cowshed or suspended in the farmhouse chimney. The reasons behind this belief seem to lie in the ancient pagan idea of blood sacrifice producing greater fertility.

Seeing a white horse is bad luck

If someone encounters a white horse, especially on the way to a funeral, superstition dictates that they should spit to dispel any bad luck this may bring. Some versions of this belief state that spitting on the finger or sole of the shoe is enough, while others dictate that it is the horse itself that must be spat on. There is plenty of evidence for this practice being widespread in the nineteenth and early twentieth centuries, and sometimes the aversion extended to grey horses or to piebald, or partly white, horses. However, as with many superstitions, contradictory beliefs also existed, and it was common in some districts for children to count white horses as they saw them, and make a wish when they reached a hundred.

In the days before motorised transport, horses

were a treasured and valuable possession, and much folklore surrounded them. For a horse to stumble at the outset of a journey was considered a very bad omen, and travellers would sometimes turn back rather than risk venturing further. Horses were also believed to be particularly susceptible to witchcraft, and a horse who refused to work or even move was often thought to have been bewitched. And should one be found in a locked stable in the morning, covered in sweat and in a nervous, excitable state, it had undoubtedly been 'hag-ridden' by witches.

Hedgehogs steal cows' milk

Implausible as it may seem, the belief that hedgehogs were able to suck the milk from cows' udders was widespread in farming communities until well into the twentieth century. Cows that were found to have blood in their milk were thought to have been the victim of hedgehogs, and the creatures were officially declared vermin as a result.

Moles' feet are lucky

The distinctive large front feet of a mole were

once seen as bringing good fortune and health, and it was not uncommon for people to hang them around the neck as a charm. Worn in this way, they were thought to cure toothache and other ailments. Unluckily for the poor mole, however, an old wives' tale also insisted that the feet should be removed while it was still alive and that the creature should then be left to die in its own time.

A related superstition stated that someone who captured a mole and then held the animal until it died would enjoy good fortune.

Adders are deaf

The idea that adders are deaf has no basis in fact, but seems to have originated from English translations of the Bible, which contains a mention of 'the deaf adder' in Psalm 58. Other superstitions involving snakes state that they cannot die in daylight, and that the first one seen in a year should be killed for luck. Snakeskin was often seen as having supernatural properties, and was sometimes worn inside a hat to protect the wearer from bad fortune.

Cocks crowing out of season

The crowing of cocks is traditionally seen as a good sign, since it heralds the morning and banishes the darkness. For this reason they are considered the enemy of evil, and their crowing on the day of judgement will reputedly be the fanfare that wakes the dead. At any time other than early morning, however, the crowing of a cock is a sign of forthcoming events, and may be ominous. Crowing on the doorstep indicates the arrival of a visitor, for instance. Heard in the early evening it indicates rough weather to come, and at night it is said to portend a death in the family. According to one custom, if it is heard crowing after dark the bird's feet must be felt. If they were warm to the touch then all was well, but if they were cold the cock was immediately slaughtered to avert bad luck.

The crowing of a female chicken means that misfortune is certain, and such unlucky creatures were usually put to death straight away since superstition dictates that crowing hens are unnatural and even associated with evil. A well-known rhyme tells that 'A whistling woman and a crowing hen are neither fit for God nor men'. The fear of crowing chickens is an old one, and is found in the writings of Ancient Rome.

Never bring a peacock feather indoors

Having a peacock feather in the house brings bad luck, and according to some superstitions means that any unmarried female is destined to be an old maid. Actors are particularly wary in this respect, and consider that peacock feathers will bring disaster on a performance. This old wives' tale is about 150 years old, and is probably related to the distinctive 'eyes' on a peacock's plumage. In some variations of the superstition, such feathers are ominous because they act as spies, invading the privacy of the home.

Hairs from a donkey cure disease

The hairs from a donkey's back are supposed to possess special properties, and may cure ailments, particularly whooping cough and measles in children. The hairs are usually worn round the neck in a silk bag until health is restored. In alternative versions of this superstition, the sufferer must either be passed over and under the donkey a certain number of times, or sat on its back and ridden around in circles. Sometimes it is recommended that three hairs be finely chopped and fed to an ill child in bread and butter. Such folk remedies are related to the distinctive cross-shaped marking on a donkey's back. The holy sign reputedly commemorates Jesus's entry into Jerusalem on Palm Sunday, riding on a donkey.

Handling a caterpillar

Handling a caterpillar is reputed to bring bad luck. This is especially true if it circles around someone's finger since this augurs their imminent death. Bad luck can be averted by throwing the caterpillar over the left shoulder, according to some sources. This superstition can be traced back to the seventeenth century, although the reasons why such an inoffensive creature should be a bad omen are less clear. Possibly the rash caused by some species of hairy caterpillar make them the object of suspicion.

Killing a spider is unlucky

Spiders are considered auspicious creatures in many old wives' tales, and to kill one is to court bad fortune. This may be because they prey on other insects and thus are useful to have around the home. It may also be because of the special powers attributed to spiders' webs. Cobwebs are reputed to stop bleeding if applied to a wound and, according to folklore, the humble spider protected the infant Jesus from discovery by King Herod's men by weaving a web to hide him. There are some circumstances in which killing a spider is lucky, however. Worn in a bag around the neck, for instance, a decomposing spider may cure disease. A small black variety called the money spider is reputed to bring wealth to whoever it crawls on, but even more so if it is eaten – there's one to try at home!

A bird flying into the house brings bad luck
Should a bird fly in through an open window it is a sign of bad fortune. This belief has been common since the nineteenth century and sometimes extended to birds' eggs which, if collected by children, were not brought indoors. Even today, some people will not have crockery decorated with pictures of birds in their house for fear of bringing bad luck. The origins of this are obscure, but it is probably related to the

idea that birds are embodiments of the souls of dead people.

Finding a ladybird brings luck
Should you be lucky enough to come across a ladybird, on no account should it be killed. Instead, it should be set free with the rhyme:

Ladybird, ladybird, fly away home,
Your house is on fire and your children are gone.

There have been several variations on this rhyme in existence since the Victorian era. In some alternative versions the ladybird is associated with romance, and is asked to 'tell me where my love can be!', after which the next person on whom it lands is a future husband or wife.

Ravens in the Tower of London
If the ravens leave the Tower of London, the monarchy will fall, so superstition has it. In many cultures, the raven is said to have foresight, and in the book of Genesis it acts as a messenger, bringing Noah bad news. It is not surprising, then, that the ravens, as predictors of tragedy, are an

indicator of the fate of the monarchy. However, another possible origin of this tale is not a bird but the hero of Welsh folklore Bran the Blessed. Bran translates as 'raven', and according to legend the head of this fierce warrior is buried on Tower Hill, facing and deterring potential invaders from across the Channel.

Handling a toad causes warts

This belief is quite recent, and there is little evidence of it existing in former times. Although there is no truth in it, it is linked to the rumour that toads have poisonous skin, and in fact some species do secrete acid if threatened. Older superstitions about toads stress their medicinal properties, and they were often used in folk remedies. One grisly cure recommends that a live toad be put in a bag and hung around the neck of a sick person. As the toad dies and then decomposes, it is said that the health of the wearer would return. In another case a live toad is tied to the head to cure a headache: whether the embarrassment caused by this outweighed the pain of the affliction is not documented. However, the toad's most valuable medicinal power lies in a mysterious stone that was believed to sit between its eyes. Dating back 2,000 years, this 'toadstone' was much sought after for its magical properties, and was thought among other things to repel poison. It also conferred on its owner a supernatural ability to command horses.

Babies are delivered by storks

This popular old wives' tale is of quite recent origin, but comes from older beliefs linking storks to childbirth and the family. A monogamous and faithful bird, the stork is rumoured to have a special emotional bond with its children, and to weep human tears if it is hurt. Should a stork build a nest on your roof, it is a sign of contented and prosperous domestic life. If it moves, however, the opposite is true. If a couple see a stork, they are sure to conceive a child, and in the event that a woman sees two storks she will shortly be pregnant. The stork's close association with childbirth may also be to do with its watery habitat, since in some traditions the souls of the unborn are reputed to live in water.

Howling dogs are a death omen

A howling dog has been considered a sign of ill fortune since at least the Middle Ages, and is mentioned in Shakespeare's *Henry VI* as a bad omen. In the last 300 years, it has become associated specifically with death, especially if it occurs at night. A dog howling three times followed by abrupt silence is supposed to indicate that a death has just taken place, and according to some old wives' tales the direction of the dog's tail points out where the dead person lies. Dogs are well known for their acute sense of smell and hearing, and in many superstitions such heightened senses attune them to supernatural and ghostly presences to which humans are impervious.

To stop a dog howling and possibly avert disaster, superstitions recommend taking off the left shoe, spitting on the sole, and placing it upside down.

A rabbit's foot brings good luck

A rabbit's foot is one of the best-known good-luck charms, and is still in common usage today. Seen as a symbolic guard against evil spirits, it is sometimes hung over a cot to protect a sleeping baby. The famous diarist Samuel Pepys carried a rabbit's foot as a cure for colic, and as far back as the sixteenth century it was considered to be a reliable remedy for rheumatism and other ailments. However, its current use as a lucky talisman is of much more recent origin, probably coming from the USA in the twentieth century.

Many related superstitions of an older origin state that the rabbit in general is a lucky creature. On the first morning of the month repeating the phrase 'white rabbits' three times can ensure good fortune. They are often said to have the power of the 'evil eye' since the young are born with eyes open, and are therefore reputed to be able to see and ward off malign spirits. And of course that which rabbits are renowned for, their rapid breeding, is a sign of prosperity and fortune.

Animals kneel on Christmas Eve

A festive old wives' tale has it that cattle and other farm animals kneel on Christmas Eve, just as their forebears did in the stable before the infant Jesus. Sometimes they are said to turn to the east, and in some versions of the story they even acquire the power of speech. For humans to try to witness this moment is sacrilege, however, and could result in divine punishment in the form of death. Doubtless the tale originates in the Victorian era, when sentimental nativity scenes depicted animals bowing in reverence.

CHAPTER SEVEN:
THE BODY

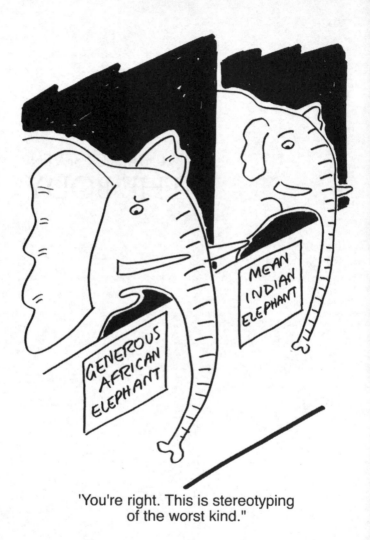

"You're right. This is stereotyping of the worst kind."

Having big ears means you are generous!

THE BODY

Birthmarks

Like any 'unusual' signs on the body, birthmarks in the past were thought to be the work of evil that the mother had done or been exposed to during pregnancy. In some societies, however, to be born with a birthmark is thought to be a lucky omen, a mark made by God on the baby's body. One superstition suggested that, if a baby's mother licked the baby's birthmark regularly, it would disappear. It was also common to encourage mothers to rub black pepper on their skin during pregnancy to make sure the baby was not born with any marks on their own skin.

Ears

There are several common superstitions associated with the ears. Large ears are considered by popular lore to be clear indicators of a person's superior generosity; by contrast, those with small ears are considered ungenerous and unkind. There are also superstitions regarding the shape of the ears: if they are square, ears are signs of nobility; if they are flat, their owner is not thought to be particularly refined; if they are long, it is a sign of wisdom. A person who feels their ears twitching or itching can be certain that somebody somewhere is talking about them. Whether what is being said is good or bad depends on which ear is affected: if it is the right ear, something good is being said; if it is the left, it is probably bad and slanderous gossip.

Eyebrows

A person whose eyebrows meet is supposedly very untrustworthy. In the past the joined eyebrows were thought to be markings from the Devil, and those who had joining eyebrows were thought to be werewolves or witches. Other superstitions, however, saw joined eyebrows as lucky signs, especially if they appeared on women, who were then said to be destined to have a happy marriage. The origin of this superstition is hard to trace, but we can reasonably speculate that it is based on the relatively rare nature of this trait. Like being left-handed, having joined eyebrows could appear to be a sign of 'difference', which could give the bearer special – possibly sinister – powers.

Excrement

In the seventeenth century there was a proverb that said that 'muk is luk', suggesting that excrement was lucky. In many places it is considered good luck to step on excrement. The origins of this belief are unknown but it seems likely that the superstition arose simply to cheer up those who had the misfortune of getting their feet stuck on such unpleasant matter. In Italy and other places in southern Europe, it is thought that to dream about excrement is a sign that money is on its way. Popular dream interpretation worked by associations, which either went by analogy (for example to have a dream of something wet like rain could mean tears) or by opposites. Thus, something disgusting and expelled and rejected by the body like excrement would transform, once the dreamer was awake, into something pleasant to be savoured and welcomed. It is also possible that money and excrement were linked by analogy as well, both being considered 'dirty' by Christian society.

The evil eye

The idea that harm may be caused by looking at somebody is an extremely ancient belief that stretches across Europe and the Middle East. It can be traced back to at least AD 1000, but it is probably even more ancient. People with blue or green eyes were the most likely to cause evil by looking (or so it was thought, especially in areas around the Mediterranean where such colours were rarer than darker eyes). The belief in the evil eye is deeply connected with witchcraft and, as with witchcraft, it would often bring suspicion on to weaker elements of society: the elderly, gypsies, women (especially unmarried women or widows). These people were usually suspected of giving the evil eye when they had been slighted or mistreated. It was also thought that boasting of one's good fortune could attract the evil eye, since it was often associated with envy. During times of heightened mass hysteria concerning witchcraft it became very dangerous to praise people or things while looking at them because such praises could be interpreted as being masked curses accompanying the evil eye. For the same reason, pointing at things was also a dangerous act, as it could also be interpreted as a way of focusing evil energy on to things.

There were many ways of warding off the evil eye and some of these practices continue today. The most powerful centre around the amulets made of blue and white glass and representing an actual eye that can be found in Turkey and all over the Middle East. It is common to place these amulets on to doorways, usually facing outwards. It is also common in the rest of Europe to have silver or iron charms in bracelets or necklaces made in the shape of eyes. Red ribbons were also traditionally used as protection against the evil eye, and it was common to tie such ribbons around purses and baby cradles for protection. There were also gestures that one could make for protection against the evil eye, especially when boasting or exposing one's riches and good fortune. The most basic of these gestures was making the sign of the cross, or the 'Devil's horns' (clenching the two middle fingers against the palm and stretching out index finger and pinkie) pointing downwards or towards the person thought to be making the evil eye.

Red hair
People with red hair were traditionally considered hot-tempered, overly sensual, dangerous, cruel and unlucky. It was thought unlucky to see a red-haired person in the morning, especially if it was a woman. Redheads in general were to be avoided at the beginning of any new project or endeavour, or at the start of the New Year. It was also considered particularly dreadful for a person to have a red beard, and for that reason many historical villains were depicted with a red beard, the most famous of all probably being Judas Iscariot. There were many superstitious explanations about the causes of red hair: some thought it was a marker of a woman's infidelity to her husband; others believed it was the result of having had intercourse during menstruation. It was also widely held in Britain that those with red

hair were descendants of the Danes, thus partially enemy folk.

The origins of these prejudices towards red-haired people can be traced to the relative rarity of the genetic trait and to the power associated with the colour red, which was seen as having supernatural properties due to its association with the colour of blood. For that very reason, red is often the chosen colour to wear in religious ceremonies, and red-headed people may have been considered dangerous precisely because the colour of their hair possessed a sacred quality.

Sneezing and 'God bless you!'

The custom of saying 'God bless you!' when a person sneezes is partially due to superstition. Many sources claim that this expression dates back to the Great Plague when the fear of contagion was very widespread and counter-expressions were devised to ward off evil and disease. This theory is contradicted by records of such an expression appearing already in ancient times, and by the fact that the main symptoms of the Great Plague were buboes (large blisters on the body, usually appearing along lymph nodes), rashes and high fever rather than sneezing. In the ancient world, it was thought that sneezing marked the visitation of a god who may have temporarily possessed the body of the sneezer or simply made his presence felt. 'God bless you' then would not have been an expression of pity or shock as it is usually interpreted to be today, but rather a statement: 'God blesses you.' Already in Ancient Rome this initial positive interpretation of the visitation of a god was turned into a negative omen, and Romans usually said *absit omen* – 'banish the omen' – when a person sneezed, hoping to reverse any negative meaning implied in the sneeze (usually serious illness and death).

Right vs left hand
According to superstition, the right hand is the hand of God while the left hand is the hand of the Devil. For this reason, left-handed people were regarded with scorn and dread in the past, and left-handed children were forced to write with their right hand in the hope that they might 'learn' to become right-handed. This superstition around the left and right sides of the body can be linked to very ancient beliefs about a world

divided in clear and polar opposites (male and female, light and dark, strong and weak) where the left hand was linked with all negative things. Ritual oaths and gestures were always performed with the right hand, and evil spirits, witches and demons were always confronted with a raised right hand, perhaps while drawing the sign of the cross in the air. For the same reasons amulets depicting hands are always carved in the shape of a right, not a left, hand. Another superstition surrounding hands is that if they itch this is an omen. If the right hand itches, it is a sign that money is on the way. If the left hand itches, it is thought that one is going to lose money. So, if both of your hands are itching simultaneously, respond with indifference!

Menstruating women are dangerous
Beyond the modern references to PMT and 'the time of the month', there are taboos and superstitions surrounding the presence of menstruating women during rituals and around food in almost all societies. This fear of menstruating women may stem from the fact that they bleed profusely without dying or

experiencing excessive pain, something that must have appeared mysterious and powerful to primitive societies. The correspondence of the female cycle with the same number of days as the phases of the moon also contributed to the sense that menstruating women were magical and sinister. The Bible explicitly states that menstruating women are considered 'unclean' and must be isolated for seven days during their period, and many other societies from Africa to North America also isolated women during that time. In Islam, menstruating women are exempt from celebrating Ramadan. In many societies they were not allowed to prepare food as it was thought they might contaminate it and perhaps cause illness or death for those consuming such meals. Menstruating women were thought to damage crops and anything that grows – probably because menstruation is the opposite of pregnancy – and they were barred from coming into contact with such substances as milk, eggs and seeds, all of which were seen to be symbols of life and growth. In Roman times menstruating women were thought to make trees drop their fruit and plants die, so they were not allowed near fields and crops.

These superstitious and misogynous beliefs have receded, but echoes of them still remain: menstruating women are thought not to be able to get mayonnaise to emulsify or jam to congeal!

Nails and hair

There are many superstitions surrounding nails and hair, since these were thought to be particularly vulnerable to spells because they were extensions of a person's body that could be used for evil if they fell into the wrong hands. Pieces of nails and hair, in fact, were very common ingredients in both evil spells and love potions. It was common in the past to burn clipped nails and hair so as to prevent witches from using them. The nails of small children would normally be kept in a safe place in the house or burned, and mothers were discouraged from cutting their children's nails until their first birthday so as to prevent their children from dying an early death or being replaced by changelings (see entry on page 183).

There were also many superstitions surrounding the appropriate days of the week to clip nails. In ancient times it was considered lucky to cut nails on Tuesday, and this superstition continued until the early fifteenth century. Later that century, writers suggested that it was unlucky to cut nails on Friday and Sunday. This belief can be easily linked to the Christian tradition, Friday being the day Jesus Christ was crucified, a day when it is unlucky to eat meat and to perform any activity that may be reminiscent of that death, and Sunday being the day of the Lord when the Resurrection took place, as well as the recommended day of rest. Perhaps cutting nails was considered work; perhaps it was a gesture linked to death since it was about severing parts of the body; either way these acts were considered inappropriate for a Sunday. There is also an old rhyme associated with the days of the week best suited for cutting nails:

Cut them on Monday, you cut them for health
Cut them on Tuesday, you cut them for wealth
Cut them on Wednesday, you cut them for news
Cut them on Thursday, a new pair of shoes
Cut them on Friday, you cut them for sorrow
Cut them on Saturday, your true love tomorrow
Cut them on Sunday, the Devil will be with you all the week.

Teeth

To dream about losing teeth was once thought to be a bad omen predicting a death in the family. The origins of this belief are unclear though very ancient, appearing in the written record as far back as AD 1050. If a baby was born with teeth, this was considered a terrible omen of bad things to come. This belief dates back to very ancient times, already being written about as early as 77 BC. Because teething is a particularly traumatic time in the life of infants, who are sometimes in great pain and may transform from calm babies to angry little screamers, there are a lot of superstitions surrounding teething. As soon as a child began teething, it was important to rub the gums with salt to protect the child from evil. There was also the practical benefit, of course, of disinfecting the child's gums. It was considered unlucky to start teething early, as this was seen to announce an early death, though to start teething from the bottom was seen to be a sign of longevity. Milk teeth were normally burned and there was a superstition, dating back to the early nineteenth century, that, if baby teeth came into the possession of an animal, the child would grow animal teeth instead of human ones. A gap in the two front teeth was thought to bring riches or a wealthy marriage.

CHAPTER EIGHT:
LOVE AND MARRIAGE

On their wedding night, the last one of the couple to go to sleep will live longer…

LOVE AND MARRIAGE

Love divination

According to superstition, the true feelings of a loved one can be ascertained by plucking the petals of a daisy one by one while reciting the phrase 'He loves me, he loves me not'. The last petal determines whether or not passion is reciprocated (see page 287). In a related custom, a single woman may pick a handful of daisies with her eyes closed, and the number of flowers she holds is said to correspond to the number of years remaining until she marries. The origin of these practices is not clear, but they seem to date from the Victorian period, and are possibly related to the daisy's associations of purity and simplicity.

Such an unassuming flower could be relied upon to tell the truth.

Apples are also commonly used in love divination, and are said to reveal the identity of a future spouse. An unmarried woman may discover her future husband by peeling the skin from an apple in one piece and tossing it over her left shoulder. If the peel forms a letter, it will be the initial of the man she is to marry. Should it break into pieces, however, she is destined to remain unmarried. The pips of an apple may also be named after prospective lovers and stuck on to the cheek. The last one to fall represents a true love. In another apple-divination custom, the apple is held and its stalk twisted while reciting the letters of the alphabet. The stalk is said to break at the initial of a future lover. Apples seem to have a special connection with love and matrimony, possibly because they are often seen as the 'forbidden fruit' plucked from the tree of knowledge, for eating which Adam and Eve were expelled from Paradise. Thus, they not only represent the revealing of knowledge, they are also associated with the loss of innocence and implicitly with sex.

A kiss from a dark man means a wedding

It is said that the girl who is kissed by a man with a dark complexion will soon receive a proposal of marriage, possibly from the man himself. Less fortunate is the girl who kisses a moustachioed man and finds a stray hair on her lip as a result, since she is destined to be a spinster. Kissing has long been considered a significant or even magical act, since a meeting of breaths symbolises a meeting of spirits. However, to kiss someone over their shoulder from behind is unlucky, and indicates deceitfulness or betrayal.

Women may only propose on 29 February

The last day of February in a leap year is known as the day on which tradition may be reversed and women are permitted to propose marriage to their hesitant lovers. The originator of this is reputed to be the Irish St Bridget, who complained to St Patrick that women were often forced to wait too long for reluctant men to pop the question. As a result, Patrick granted the opportunity once every four years for women to take the initiative.

Engagement

When considering proposing marriage, a suitor should choose the setting carefully since a proposal should not take place on a train or bus, or in public view, according to superstition. And, when shopping for an engagement ring, the selection of a stone is important. Diamonds, sapphires, emeralds and rubies are all considered lucky, but pearls are to be avoided since they symbolise tears. The day of the week on which the ring is bought may be taken as an indication of the nature of the marriage ahead. Monday means an eventful married life, while Tuesday indicates contentment, Wednesday portends harmony and Thursday means that wishes will be fulfilled. Friday indicates that the couple will have to strive to achieve their goals, whereas Saturday indicates instead a life of pleasure.

For the ring to be adjusted is an inauspicious sign, and equally unlucky is for anyone apart from the bride to try it on. However, they may slip it on the very end of their finger and make a wish.

Once engaged, the couple should try to avoid having their photo taken together and should take great care when choosing their wedding day, since it is extremely bad luck to change it. The reading of the banns, indicating their intention to marry, should take place on three consecutive Sundays, but the couple must not attend since one old wives' tale states that their children will be born deaf and dumb as a result. Once the final reading has taken place, the wedding cannot be called off without risking great misfortune.

Should she get cold feet, however, the nervous bride-to-be may end the engagement by presenting her fiancé with the gift of a knife, presumably a symbol of the severing of their attachment. She should take care in doing this, though, since after three terminated engagements it is said that the Devil may claim your soul!

Choosing a day

Although Saturdays are now the most popular day for weddings, they were considered unlucky in the past, and an old rhyme advises marriage only in the first half of the week:

Monday for health,
Tuesday for wealth,

Wednesday best of all,
Thursday for losses,
Friday for crosses,
Saturday for no luck at all.

Sunday was considered to be the luckiest day of the week on which to be married, since it was the most sacred.

Similarly, while May weddings are now fairly common, it was once thought to be the most inauspicious of all months to be married: 'Marry in the month of May, and you'll surely rue the day'. In Victorian times, fear of May weddings was such that vicars were inundated with requests to be married before the start of the unlucky month, and Queen Victoria herself is said to have banned her children from marrying in May. While the origins of this idea are not clear, one theory is that it dates from pre-Christian times when the start of summer was associated with the feast of Beltane and its orgiastic revelries, and such celebrations were not an appropriate backdrop for the start of married life. An alternative theory suggests the idea originated in Ancient Rome, where the feast of the dead and the festival of the goddess of chastity both occurred in May. To avoid a wedding associated with death or chastity, ancient Romans married in June instead, which was the month of the goddess Juno, protector of women and matrimony.

Advent and Lent are to be avoided when scheduling a wedding, the latter presumably because it was supposed to be a time of abstinence and penitence rather than feasting and celebration. It is considered inadvisable to get married on your birthday, or in the dark. Superstition about the timing of weddings also dictates that to be married under a waxing moon is lucky, and in coastal districts it was also common to time a marriage to correspond with the tide, which should be on the way in rather than out. Both of these, obviously, symbolise growth and prosperity.

The morning of the wedding

On the morning of the wedding, it is considered lucky for the bride to feed the family cat before she sets off for the church, although the origins of this superstition are a mystery. The same goes for the belief that the front doorstep should be washed before the wedding party leaves the house, since the bridesmaid who wets the hem of her dress by walking on it improves her chances of marriage.

On the way to the church

Superstition has it that seeing a chimneysweep on the way to the wedding brings good luck, and it is not unknown nowadays for couples to hire one to attend the ceremony. The idea dates back to the reign of George II, whose life was saved by a passing sweep who managed to bring the runaway royal carriage to a halt. The monarch showed his gratitude by bowing low before the man, and henceforth declaring all chimneysweeps to be lucky. More recently, newspapers reported that another royal, Prince Philip, spied a chimneysweep from his window in Kensington Palace on the morning of his wedding to Queen Elizabeth, and rushed out to shake hands and ensure good luck.

Other harbingers of marital bliss are lambs, black cats, rainbows, toads and spiders. In the unlikely event that the wedding party should encounter an elephant on the way to the church, they will be especially fortunate. Conversely, bad omens include seeing a pig or a lizard. Seeing a nun or monk is also considered to be bad luck, because it hints that the impending union may either be childless or dependent on charity. And, perhaps unsurprisingly, the sight of an open grave connotes death, as does meeting a funeral party en route to the wedding.

On the way to the church, the wedding party should not cross running water, and in a variation on the New Year 'first-footing' ritual (see page 233), the groom should traditionally present the first person he meets on his way with a coin. On leaving the church, the couple must take a different route back, since in the days of horse-drawn carriages it was considered bad luck to turn the horses around. Instead, they must continue in the same direction, and find a circular route home.

Weather on the wedding day
Weather is considered to be an important indicator of the marriage to come. 'Blessed is the

bride the sun shines on', as the saying has it. Snow is likewise an auspicious sign, and is linked to fertility and happiness. Rain is considered a bad sign, portending a stormy marriage. It may be that rain was bad for more practical reasons in former times, however, since marriages were usually carried out at the church door, rather than inside the building itself.

The wedding dress
There are many old wives' tales attached to the subject of wedding outfits, particularly that of the bride. For the bride to wear her entire outfit before the wedding day is considered unlucky, as is the groom seeing the bride in her dress prior to the ceremony. Marrying in white, a colour traditionally symbolising purity, is supposedly auspicious but is a relatively modern custom. Queen Victoria may have popularised the white wedding dress in the 1840s, but it wasn't until much more recently that ordinary people could afford such a luxurious item. Most people merely wore their best clothes to be married in, irrespective of colour. However, a green dress was to be avoided at all costs. The rhyme 'Married in

green, ashamed to be seen' indicates the negative connotations of this colour; 'having a green gown' meant having loose morals, a belief possibly linked to telltale grass stains on a woman's dress. Other theories suggest that the colour green should be avoided for different reasons. It is a colour bound to attract pixies, sprites and other malevolent wood spirits, possibly causing the green-clad bride to be carried off by the 'little people'! In some cases, this superstition is taken as far as banning the inclusion of green vegetables at the wedding banquet.

Silk is considered the luckiest fabric for a wedding dress, while satin brings misfortune and velvet is to be avoided since it means a marriage of poverty.

The bridal veil
The wearing of a bridal veil has a much older origin than the wedding dress, and goes back as far as Roman times. While it indicated modesty and chastity, it was also considered to fulfil a more practical function, in that it would disguise the bride and thus outwit any evil spirits who might wish to prey on her. It has been suggested that bridesmaids,

dressed similarly to the bride, were also traditionally intended to confuse malevolent spirits.

Something old, something new, something borrowed, something blue

This popular rhyme, indicating four objects to be included in the bride's ensemble for good luck, did not become well known until the twentieth century and probably originated in Victorian times. Traditionally, 'something old' should be a handkerchief or shoes, and is thought to signify continuity and permanence in terms of the couple's friends. However, in an alternative version of the custom, this can be an old garter given to the bride by a happily married woman so that she might enjoy an equally successful and happy marriage. 'Something new' symbolises a healthy and prosperous future for the couple. 'Something borrowed' is commonly an object of value lent by the bride's family, which must be returned to ensure good luck. A variation on the rhyme replaces something borrowed with 'something golden' or 'something stolen'. 'Something blue' is thought to be fortunate because the colour represents faithfulness and constancy. Chaucer's *Squire's Tale* contains a reference to the wearing of blue to symbolise fidelity, for instance; and in Ancient Hebrew custom, brides reputedly wore a blue ribbon in their hair for the same reason. The rhyme sometimes finishes with the line 'and a silver sixpence in her shoe', and accordingly a coin is placed in the bride's shoe. This is commonly thought to symbolise wealth in married life, but in the oldest recorded versions of the custom, dating from the late seventeenth century, the coin is intended to ward off evil spirits.

Tying the knot

The phrase 'to tie the knot' may now be merely a figure of speech, indicating a metaphorical bonding together of the married couple, but in former times it had a literal significance. Marriage ceremonies hundreds of years ago used to involve the symbolic tying together of threads from the couple's clothes, or else the binding of their thumbs or fingers. In India, this practice still carries on, and in Hindu weddings the bride's and groom's wrists are linked together with twine soaked in turmeric water for luck.

Names

According to superstition, it is considered bad luck for the bride's maiden name to have the same initial as the groom's surname:

Change the name, not the letter,

Change for the worse, and not for the better.

Even more unlucky is for the wife-to-be to practise using her married name prior to the wedding. To avoid tempting fate, it was common in the past to label marriage linen with her maiden name.

Giving away the bride

A traditional feature of wedding ceremonies is for the bride to be 'given away' by a male relative, typically her father. While this is now merely symbolic, it has its roots in former ages when a bride passed from the authority of her father to that of her new husband during marriage. The transfer of 'ownership' was often facilitated by the payment of a dowry – a sum of money or goods – which the groom would pay to the family of the bride in exchange for her hand in marriage.

Wedding rings

The wedding ring is an ancient and important emblem of marital union, the circle symbolising unity and eternity, and accordingly many superstitions are connected to it. It is considered bad luck for the bride to wear the ring before her marriage, for instance. Dropping the wedding ring during the ceremony is also considered highly unlucky, and it is even believed that whichever of the couple is guilty of such a fumble will die first. In the event that it *is* dropped, however, neither the bride nor groom should retrieve it, but the minister officiating at the service. It is generally considered bad luck to remove a wedding ring, the symbolism of this being obvious, but according to some superstitions it can safely be taken off after the birth of the first child. Such is its symbolic potency, it is sometimes used in divining rituals: the sex of an unborn child can be determined by observing the direction of its swing, for instance, and an unmarried woman may sleep with one under her pillow to dream of her future husband. Should a wedding ring become so worn and thin that it breaks, however, the death of one of the couple may be imminent.

Wedding rings are used in different forms in many different cultures, but in the British Isles they have traditionally taken the form of a plain gold band. In former times, when couples could not afford gold, a cheaper metal, typically iron, was used. If even this was beyond the couple's means, it was acceptable for the bride to put her finger though the loop in the church key in the absence of a ring.

The practice of wearing the wedding ring on the fourth finger of the left hand is an old one, and dates back to classical times when a vein was supposed to run directly from the ring finger to the heart, connecting it with matters of love and matrimony. In other parts of Europe, however, it is conventional to wear the ring on the fourth finger of the right hand, rather than the left. The first three digits supposedly symbolise the Holy Trinity, whereas the fourth may be used for earthly union.

Wedding curses

While most of those attending a wedding undoubtedly wish the couple well, it is supposedly possible for disgruntled guests to curse the marriage by tying a knot in a piece of string or a handkerchief three times, as the priest reads the service. This results, reputedly, in a childless marriage for the first fifteen years, unless the piece of string is ceremonially burned.

When choosing the readings, Psalm 109 is to be avoided, as this similarly brings bad luck on a marriage.

Crying at the wedding

The stress of the big day means it is not uncommon for the bride to shed a few tears at her wedding. Contradictory superstitions surround crying at a marriage. According to some, it is a good sign, indicating happiness in the future since all tears have been symbolically shed before married life begins. Others insist it is an indication of the stormy nature of the marriage to come. It may once have had another significance, however. Some sources argue that since a witch was reputedly unable to cry more than three tears, it was auspicious for a bride to weep at her wedding since it proved she was not a witch!

Leaving the church

Guests should keep a keen eye out to see which of the married couple sets foot outside the church first after the ceremony. Custom says that, if it is the woman, she will be the dominant partner in the marriage.

Throwing confetti

Tossing confetti over the married couple as they emerge from the church is traditionally intended to bring them luck, and close examination of the little pieces of paper reveal they are made up of horseshoes and other good luck symbols. However, confetti itself is a recent introduction to weddings, presumably from Italy where the word means 'sweeties' and refers to confectionery thrown in the air at carnival time. Until well into the twentieth century, it was rice, or occasionally nuts, that was tossed over the bride and groom. And tracing the practice back even further, before rice was common in British kitchens, couples would be showered with wheat. Records show that Henry VII received this treatment at his nuptials, and it appears to date back even further than this, possibly to

Roman times. The choice of wheat probably relates to fertility and growth, and is therefore symbolically intended to encourage the couple to have children.

Catching the bride's bouquet

After the wedding, the bride tosses her bouquet over her shoulder towards the bridesmaids and unmarried female guests, and custom dictates that the one to catch it will be next to marry. While this practice is a fairly recent American import, having only spread to Britain in the last forty years or so, it does seem to mirror some older superstitions. The bridal bouquet has long been considered to bring luck, so much so that in the past guests would scramble for pieces of it even before the ceremony began. However, the object that was originally thrown after the wedding was not the bride's bouquet, but her stocking. Records show that in Tudor England it was customary for the bride to remove her left stocking, before flinging it over her right shoulder to determine who would be next up the aisle. In some cases, guests would accompany the newlywed couple back to their marriage

117

chamber and take turns in throwing the bride's stockings from the foot of the bed. If a stocking landed on the head of the hapless groom, its thrower would be certain to marry next. By the time of Queen Victoria, such bawdy activities were frowned on and the bride's stocking was replaced first by her shoe and eventually by the altogether more refined bouquet. However, the original custom is still sometimes echoed today in the tossing of the garter, a practice widespread in the USA. This is a parallel to the tossing of the bouquet in which the groom removes the bride's garter and throws it to the single male guests.

Wedding presents

The custom of giving presents to the new couple dates back to Roman times, when they were presented with fruit, symbolising fertility. Nowadays, gifts tend to be more expensive, but it is best to avoid giving knives, as this is very inauspicious and is a harbinger of a rocky marriage!

Wedding cake

The wedding cake is an important part of the marriage celebrations, and many superstitions surround it. Traditionally, it is supposed to be made of the richest ingredients available in order to symbolise a prosperous marriage, but the bride should take no part in baking it, nor should she taste it before the day of the wedding. Bride and groom are supposed to cut the cake together as an indication of their partnership and the sharing of tasks in married life. Everyone present should eat a piece of the cake, since to refuse is bad luck. In former times, it was customary either to crumble a piece of the cake over the bride's head, or else to throw bits of it at the couple!

After the wedding day, it is said that the bride should keep a slice of the cake to ensure the faithfulness of her husband in years to come, and many couples preserve a tier of the cake for use as a christening cake. Pieces of the wedding cake were much sought after by single women, who used them in elaborate marriage divination rituals. After passing morsels of cake through the wedding ring, a single woman was required to walk backwards up to bed and sleep with the cake under her pillow. In this way, it was said, she would dream of her future husband.

Wedding cakes exist in many different cultures, and, in China, they are considered to bring luck to all involved in the wedding. In Britain, their origin can be found in 'bride cakes', buns that were brought by the guests and piled up in front of the couple at the wedding feast. The higher the stack of bride cakes, the more prosperous their future together would be.

Tying shoes to the wedding car

As the couple drive away, it is customary for their car to be followed by a trail of old shoes and, latterly, tin cans tied to the bumper by well-wishers. This strange ritual originates in the old wedding practice of 'throwing the shoe'. In Tudor times, it was common for couples to be pelted with shoes as their carriages drove away, and some sources suggest that the tradition goes back still further, to Ancient Rome.

Shoes have long been involved in other wedding superstitions. Before the advent of the custom of tossing the bouquet, it was often a shoe that was thrown to determine who would be next to the altar. And in some societies it is traditional for the husband to tap his bride on the head with his shoe. Shoes have long been a symbol of authority, which is why some religions demand their removal on entry to places of worship. This gentle tap on the head therefore indicates the husband's mastery over his new wife.

The honeymoon

The custom of the honeymoon dates back hundreds of years, to when couples were expected not to go on holiday after their wedding, but instead to drink a mixture of honey and mead for the first thirty days of their marriage. Honey was considered an aphrodisiac and was often given as a wedding gift. The thirty-day period corresponded to one full cycle of the moon, hence the word 'honeymoon'.

Carrying over the threshold

Superstition dictates that it is unlucky for a newly married woman to walk over the threshold of her home, and that she must instead be carried by her husband. This custom is probably intended to symbolise the transition to a new life, but it is possible that bride-lifting was introduced to avoid the bad fortune that would ensue if she were to stumble on her way into her new house. For the bride to trip at such an important moment would obviously be a very inauspicious sign for the marriage. It has also been argued that this practice is a relic of more barbarous times in which brides were less-than-willing partners in marriage, and were forcibly captured from neighbouring tribes by their husbands. This idea at least helps to explain the purpose of the best man who, along with the groom's friends, was enlisted to assist in the kidnap and to escort the bride to her new house. The theory seems to be supported by records of an Ancient Roman custom in which the bride was lifted bodily over the threshold by a group of men. In Britain, however, there is no evidence that the practice dates from before the early nineteenth century.

Pity the poor bride in Poland, however, where rituals surrounding the entry into the marital home are still more bemusing. Traditionally, she circled a fire three times and then bathed her feet. With a blindfold placed over her eyes, her face veiled and her mouth filled with honey, she was led over the threshold before kicking each door in turn with her right foot. Finally, the water used to wash her feet was splashed on to the marital bed to ensure good luck.

The wedding night

While sleep may not be uppermost in most couples' minds on their wedding night, they should avoid being the first to drop off, since a rather sinister superstition dictates that whoever falls asleep last will also live longer!

CHAPTER NINE:
FOOD AND DRINK

Eating the last slice of bread on the
table brings a husband or money to the
single woman!

FOOD AND DRINK

Hollow bread signifies death

Slicing a loaf of bread to find a hole in the middle is considered a very bad sign. The hollow is reputed to represent a grave or coffin, and therefore indicates that a friend or relative is soon to die. This belief was widespread in the late nineteenth century, but one variation suggests that the hole indicates a forthcoming pregnancy rather than death.

Old wives' tales concerning bread have been common for centuries. Its status as a staple food in European society, and its biblical significance, helps explain why it played such an important role in folklore and superstition. Pieces of bread were placed under a child's pillow as protection from evil, or else worn under their clothing. Unsurprising, then, that a loaf breaking apart while being cut meant bad fortune was on the way.

Don't throw crumbs on the fire

After sweeping up crumbs of bread from the floor or table, it is important not to dispose of them by throwing them on the fire, as according to superstition this feeds the Devil. Since bread is often a symbol of life, and fire is associated with hell, the logic of this old wives' tale is not hard to understand.

Never prick a loaf with a fork or knife

When pricking a loaf to test if it is thoroughly cooked, only a skewer can be used – never a knife or fork. The reasons for this are obscure, but it is one of many old wives' tales attached to the process of baking. Since bread has long been important as a symbol of life and health, it is not surprising that its production was surrounded by superstition. Bread made on a Good Friday is lucky, and marking the loaves with a cross before baking them was a common practice for hundreds of years, since it stopped the Devil 'sitting' on them. No scraps of dough should be left over or the baking will be unsuccessful, and according to some local sayings, if the cook strokes the face of a boy immediately after kneading the dough, he will be unable to grow a beard. A loaf put in to an oven upside down is unlucky and augurs death, while, if four cooked loaves are found stuck together when removed, marriage is on the cards. However, counting loaves as they are removed from the oven is to be avoided, as it brings bad luck.

Twelve for the baker and one for the Devil

The traditional 'baker's dozen' of thirteen loaves is supposed to contain an extra loaf for the Devil, a measure designed to prevent any evil finding its way into the other twelve. In actual fact, the surplus bread is to compensate for shrinkage during the baking process. A baker would add this odd loaf to any batch of a dozen to ensure a fair weight for the buyer.

The last slice of bread and butter

If a single woman takes the last slice of bread and butter from a plate, she may be given the choice between a handsome husband or £1,000 a year. This superstition is of uncertain origin, but the sum of £1,000, which has not kept pace with inflation, probably dates it to the nineteenth century. In some versions the bread must be offered to her, as otherwise she is destined to remain single.

Butter-side down
When a slice of bread is accidentally dropped, take care to notice how it lands. Butter-side down traditionally augurs bad luck, whereas the other way up means a stranger will call.

Hot cross bun kept for luck
The traditional Easter treat of hot cross buns is considered lucky. It was common practice in the nineteenth century to make a batch on Good Friday and keep one until the same time the following year. Hung in the house as a lucky talisman, it was said never to mould. Often one such bun would be given to a sailor to take on board a ship. Its holy properties as a Christian symbol were presumably intended to ensure safe passage.

Empty eggshells should be broken

Since at least Tudor times, it has been considered very bad luck to leave eggshells intact after eating the contents. Instead they were broken up, or the bottom pierced with a spoon to prevent their use in witchcraft. A widespread belief stated that witches used 'eggboats' to cause shipwrecks. By floating the empty shells in a tub of water and simulating rough seas, they would magically summon up a real storm out in the ocean.

Eggs should not be carried after sunset

It is said that eggs should not be carried into or out of a house after dark. The reasons for this are unclear, but in the nineteenth century it was taken so seriously that many people would refuse to sell their eggs after sunset for fear of bringing bad fortune on themselves. Other inexplicable egg superstitions include the prohibition on carrying eggs over running water, and burning eggshells, since this is supposed to stop a hen from laying. A double yolk usually indicates a wedding, but in some places is taken as an indication of an imminent funeral. They are considered extremely unlucky on board a ship, and even the word 'egg' was once taboo among sailors, who instead used the word 'roundabout'.

An even number of eggs is unlucky

When 'setting' eggs, or placing them under a hen to hatch, farmers' wives would always ensure there was an odd number, preferably thirteen if possible. If, however, an even number were set to hatch, it was said that the resulting chicks would all be male. This belief was remarkably common from the seventeenth century onwards, but there is evidence it existed as far back as Ancient Rome. Several other superstitions surround the hatching of eggs. They were sometimes marked with a cross to ward off evil and ensure healthy chicks. However, should a hen produce an abnormally small round egg, it should never be allowed to hatch, or it would produce a serpent, or 'cockatrice'.

Two nuts in a kernel brings luck

Someone lucky enough to crack a nutshell to find two nuts inside should eat one, but throw the other over their shoulder in order to have a wish be granted. Alternative superstitions state that, if worn around the neck, a double nut can help alleviate toothache or that, if found by a woman, such a nut means a pregnancy resulting in twins. Nuts in general are associated with babies, and a season with a plentiful nut harvest is said to mean that many births are imminent.

There are also several old wives' tales relating nuts to love and matrimony. In the days before confetti, it was customary to toss nuts (presumably small ones!) over the newly married couple at a wedding, or else to present them with a small bag of nuts. They may also be used in ascertaining whether love is reciprocated. According to Victorian superstition, two nuts should be placed next to one another in the embers of a fire and then observed. If they stay close together, the course of love will run smooth, but, if they jump apart as they burn, trouble is in store. Alternatively, a single nut could be placed in the fire, and a rhyme recited to determine the true nature of the beloved's affections:

If he loves me, pop and fly;
If he hates me, lie and die.

However, care needed to be exercised when interpreting the results of this test. One variation on this practice dictates that a nut that jumps as it burns indicates that the lover will be unfaithful!

Yeast in a dream means pregnancy
Should you have a dream involving yeast, it indicates a forthcoming pregnancy. Since yeast causes dough to rise and swell, the symbolism of this old wives' tale is fairly obvious.

Spilling salt is unlucky
As is well known, if someone is clumsy enough to spill salt, they will be the recipient of bad luck. Every grain of salt, it is said, represents a tear to be shed later. The source of this superstition is difficult to trace but it is relatively old and has been in existence in one form or another since the sixteenth century. Previous versions state that the person towards whom the salt falls will be unlucky, rather than the person who is responsible for the spill. Whatever the details, it originates in a period when salt was a much sought-after commodity, and spilling some of this precious substance would indeed be a piece of bad fortune.

However, an equally well-known superstition dictates that misfortune can be averted by immediately throwing a pinch of spilled salt over the left shoulder, supposedly because this is where the Devil traditionally perches, and the act of tossing the salt either banishes him or prevents evil thoughts being whispered into the ear. The idea that salt may be used to repel evil spirits is very old, and the book of Leviticus commands that salt should be added to offerings of grain. Bags of salt were commonly hung over a child's cradle as protection prior to its christening, and it is often used in the custom of 'first footing' to ensure good luck. Bowls of salt were also placed on a dead body, a practice seen in the eighteenth century that was intended to benefit the soul of the deceased. This has as much to do with eternal life as it does warding off evil: salt was a preservative and was used in embalming.

Other old wives' tales relating to salt state that knocking over the salt cellar means the end of a friendship. Putting salt on someone's food for them can have the same effect, as the old saying 'Help to salt, help to sorrow' indicates. Burning salt is also s bad omen; and, should a neighbour ask to borrow some, you should refuse: salt should either be given as a gift or sold, but never loaned.

Peas are lucky

The pea is considered a lucky vegetable, especially a solitary one found growing in a pod. A wish may be made while tossing a pea over the shoulder, for instance, and it is said to act as a cure for a wart if rubbed on the affected area.

Breaking the wishbone

One very well-known practice accompanying the eating of a roast fowl is the breaking of the wishbone. According to custom, two people each take hold of either side of the thin V-shaped bone and then pull it apart while making a wish. The wish of the person holding the largest part will supposedly be granted. Variations on this superstition date back to the seventeenth century when the bone was known as a 'merrythought', but in former times it was marriage rather than a wish that was at stake: it was said that the winner of the contest would be the first up the aisle. While the practice seems to have no specific source, commentators have attempted to explain it in terms of the wishbone's similarity to a horseshoe or, more confusingly, to female genitals!

Pepper is an aphrodisiac
The idea that pepper may improve one's sex drive is possibly linked to the condiment's fiery nature. A small amount sprinkled on the chair of an unwelcome guest, however, is said to cause them to leave.

Dropping a spoon
The significance of dropping a spoon depends on the way it lands. Bowl up augurs good fortune, whereas bowl down means disappointment is in store. The origin of this seems to lie in the idea that a face-down spoon must be empty. Whatever item of cutlery is dropped, however, it should always be picked up by someone other than the person responsible. Having two spoons in a cup at the same time is said to be significant, meaning either the arrival of twins or, if that person is single, an upcoming wedding. And in common with many superstitions about left-handedness, it is unlucky to use a spoon to stir with the left hand.

An eel prevents drunkenness

In order to prevent the effects of alcohol, one old wives' tale suggests that a live eel be placed into a drink. Another recommends a slightly less unappetising alternative in the shape of an owl's egg. The reason behind such superstitions is unclear, but those unable to procure – or stomach – either of these ingredients might try a pinch of rosemary, which is reputed to have much the same effect.

Garlic wards off vampires

This idea is fairly modern, and probably dates from the vampire films of the twentieth century rather than ancient folklore. However, it originates in the idea that garlic had the power to repel evil, a belief possibly linked to its potent smell. In the nineteenth century it was sometimes found hung outside houses for that reason, especially at Halloween.

Kicking over a chair betrays a lie

Carelessly kicking over a chair after a meal may reveal that the culprit has been telling lies. This old wives' tale is of uncertain origin but is probably intended to discourage bad table manners. Other superstitions about dining behaviour state that a single girl should never be sat on the corner of a table, or she will remain single. Singing at the table is also not recommended. The saying 'Sing at table, die in workhouse' was repeated to noisy children in former times. One explanation for this is that singing would attract the attention of malign spirits, and possibly culminate in destitution for the family.

Blackberries should not be picked after 10 October

It is said that Satan tumbled into a blackberry bush on this date, which in former times was Michaelmas Day. In his anger he issued a curse on it, and consequently the fruit must be harvested before 11 October. The French have also traditionally associated blackberries with the Devil, and say that their deep-red colour is that of his spit.

A joint of meat indicates fortunes

A joint of meat, should it swell while in the oven,

augurs well and indicates future prosperity. If it shrivels while cooking, however, it means that lean times are ahead. Exactly where this comes from is unknown, but the underlying symbolism of it is not difficult to decipher.

Potatoes cure rheumatism

A potato, if carried in the pocket, may relieve symptoms of rheumatism in a sufferer. However, it must be a new potato, and have been allowed to turn black and hard.

Bacon heals ailments

A rasher of bacon is said to act as a remedy for various conditions, including constipation. It is also reputed to cure warts if rubbed on the affected area. Inexplicably, however, this will be effective only if the bacon is stolen.

A stalk in tea denotes a stranger

If you find a stalk of tea floating in a cup of the beverage, a stranger is sure to call. The stalk should be fished out and placed on the back of one hand, and the wrist tapped with the other hand. The number of taps before the stalk is dislodged corresponds to the number of days before the visit. Should it feel hard to the touch, the caller will be a man; if it is soft then they will be female. If there is a possibility of romance, the stranger's true nature can be determined by placing the stalk in the palm of the hand and clapping once. If it remains, he is constant, but if it falls he is fickle and should be avoided. This rather strange procedure dates from the early Victorian period and is one of several old wives' tales about making and drinking tea, which reflect the drink's importance in British life. Like the more well-known and highly elaborate custom of reading the future in tea leaves at the bottom of the cup, however, it has largely disappeared with the advent of the teabag.

Two people should not pour from the same pot
For the same pot of tea to be poured by two different people is to court bad luck. This is especially true if they are both women. It may denote an unwelcome pregnancy, and possibly the birth of red-headed twins. This is a variation on superstitions forbidding two people to share a task, or they will soon quarrel. Other tea-pouring

old wives' tales tell that, if a man should pour more than one cup of tea for a woman, she will bear his child, and that the tea, once poured, should never be stirred anticlockwise – or 'widdershins' – as this means ill fortune. Bubbles on the surface of the tea denote either money or kisses for the drinker. All these superstitions seem to originate in the nineteenth century, when tea became a staple of the British diet.

'Cheers!'

Surely everyone at one time or another has touched their glass together with that of a fellow drinker and uttered this familiar toast. Perhaps not everyone is aware of the importance of maintaining eye contact with their drinking partner during the toast, however, since looking away is said to bring seven years of bad sex. This superstition is sometimes heard in Britain, but seems to be more widespread in parts of Europe, especially Germany.

Black pudding can foretell a marriage

According to one superstition from northern England, where black pudding has long been a delicacy, the skin on the pudding can indicate the future of a romance. The sausage-shaped pudding, made of pigs' blood, should be 'named' for a particular couple. If its skin cracks or breaks apart during cooking, their relationship is doomed, but, if it stays smooth and intact, they will be happy.

Witches can prevent butter from churning
In the days when butter was churned by hand, much significance was attached to whether the milk would 'curdle' successfully. If it failed to churn properly and turn into butter, it was a sure sign of the influence of witchcraft. For this reason, in Scotland milk churns were made out of rowan wood, a substance known to repel evil spirits. Elsewhere, the witch's spell could be removed from the milk by dropping into the churn three hairs from the tail of a black cat. Even more gruesome is the Irish custom of the 'dead hand', which involved dipping the hand of a corpse into the milk!

Spilled milk means seven days' bad luck
Be careful when pouring milk, as it is said that spilling it attracts malevolent spirits. The same

goes for allowing milk to boil over in the pan. Both these old wives' tales are of uncertain origin, but seem designed to discourage carelessness and waste. In former times, when milk was heated over an open fire, a pinch of salt thrown on to the coals while it boiled would prevent the milk yield from dwindling.

Every mince pie means a happy month
Overeating during the Christmas period may have its benefits after all, since it is said that every mince pie eaten means a trouble-free month in the year ahead. Eating twelve, therefore, ensures the following year will be a happy one, and a wish may be made while eating the first. However, some variations of this superstition dictate that each pie must be eaten in a different house, while others say they must be consumed in absolute silence. Mince pies are only propitious if eaten between Christmas Eve and Twelfth Night, however, and any eaten outside of this period may even be unlucky. Their luck-bringing properties are originally to do with their shape: before the days of factory production, mince pies would be made in a rectangular shape, considered sacred at

Christmas since it corresponded to the shape of Christ's manger. Consequently it was also bad luck to refuse one. How convenient!

Oysters are an aphrodisiac

This belief has been common since ancient times, when oysters formed a key part of the notorious orgies or bacchanalian feasts of the Romans. There is no scientific evidence for this claim – it is probably linked to the vague similarity between oysters and female genitals. It is considered unlucky to eat oysters except when there is an 'r' in the month, a superstition which made sense before the days of imported food, since it corresponded to the oyster season in Britain. More mysterious is the old wives' tale that a drop of saliva in an oyster shell may cure deafness if it is then buried in animal manure.

CHAPTER TEN:
SPORT AND PASTIMES

'Right the chicken entrails are suggesting a
2,4,4 combination and 2 substitutions at half time.'

It's amazing how superstitious
footballers can be...

SPORT AND PASTIMES

Don't swap fishing rods
Anglers who change to a different rod while fishing will find it impossible to catch a fish, according to popular angling lore. They are also advised to spit on their bait before casting a line, and not to sit on an upturned bucket while fishing. Passers-by should not ask an angler how many bites he has had, as this is a sure-fire way to stop the fish taking the bait.

A redhead at a baseball match brings luck
Baseball players, notorious for their elaborate superstitions, are convinced that the sight of a red-haired woman in the crowd brings them luck

in a game. And, traditionally, if a player managed to procure a hairpin from the woman, he would score a home run. The sight of a cross-eyed woman has the opposite effect, however, and the same goes for cross-eyed umpires, who are considered a bad omen for the match. Some players stick chewing gum on the top of their caps as it is thought to bring luck to them and their team, while others will refuse to wash their kit during a winning streak for fear of bringing it to an end. One team reportedly went for twenty-seven matches without washing their socks! Baseball players are also very reluctant to lend out their bats, as they are considered to contain only a finite number of successful strikes, which may potentially be used up by others.

The challenger must enter a boxing ring first
Boxers dislike getting into the ring before an opponent, and so the title-holder usually exercises his privilege to arrive second. Many will also take care to spit on their gloves prior to a bout because, as in many other contexts, spitting is considered lucky.

Don't restart a bowling run-up in cricket

Bowlers are reluctant to stop a run-up once it has started, since restarting is reputed to be unlucky for the fielding side. Cricketers are superstitious about many other things, too. A batsman's pads must be put on the correct legs, or he will be out for a duck, and thirteen is an unlucky score to be avoided at all costs. Two teammates will not wash their hands at the same time, since, as with many other old wives' tales involving two people doing the same task, it is said to bring bad luck. It is not only players who observe superstitions, though. The well-known umpire David Shepherd had a dread of the number 111, or 'nelsons'. If the score stood at this total, he would famously raise one leg as the ball was bowled. At 'double nelsons', or 222, he would hop so that both feet left the ground when the bowler delivered the ball!

Blowing on dice for luck

Before rolling dice, it is common to hold them in the hands and blow on them in the hope of throwing the desired number. Other superstitions state that rubbing them on a ginger-haired person may achieve the same effect.

The left football boot should be put on first
Many footballers will put their left boot on before their right as one of a number of pre-match superstitions designed to avoid bad luck. Others include a changing-room ritual of bouncing the ball between the oldest and youngest players on the team. Goalkeepers can be seen touching or kicking their posts just before the match starts, and the player about to kick off will usually bounce the ball three times on the centre spot before beginning play. Some grounds are considered luckier than others, and Derby County's Baseball Ground is said to be cursed by gypsies who were moved from it. The Italian team Napoli have possibly the most superstitious fans, who throw salt on to the pitch and bang drums and cymbals before play to scare off evil spirits.

Hunchbacks are lucky for a gambler
A gambler who sees a hunchback on the way to the casino may be in for a winning streak, but one who sees a woman should probably turn round and go home, according to gaming superstition. Gamblers also take the idea of 'beginner's luck'

seriously, and hold that a first-time player is likely to win. They are reluctant to lend money to an opponent or to play on polished tables, although the latter rule may originate in the idea that someone's cards could be seen reflected in a polished surface by other players. Someone on a losing streak should try walking around the table for luck, or perhaps sitting on a handkerchief. On no account should they sit cross-legged or pick up their cards with the left hand.

Nine of diamonds is an unlucky card

A card player dealt the nine of diamonds may feel that he will not have the best of luck. The card is known as the 'curse of Scotland' after it was used as a code by the English in 1692 to commence the Glencoe Massacre, in which many Scots were wiped out. The four of clubs is another unlucky card to be dealt in the first hand of a game, and means that all future hands will be bad ones. In poker, holding two pairs comprised of aces and eights is not desirable. This is the notorious 'dead man's hand', held by the legendary Wild Bill Hickock as he was shot dead.

Never bet on a horse whose name has been changed

There are many superstitions surrounding the sport of horseracing, and those who like a flutter often have elaborate systems for choosing a horse. However, one common rule dictates that any horse who has been renamed is sure to lose. When opting for the random method of sticking a pin in a list of horses, it is a good idea to use a pin that has been worn at a wedding.

No sex before a match

The popular theory that athletes should abstain from sex before competing in a sporting event seems to have been fairly widespread, especially in former years. The boxer Muhammad Ali would typically refrain from sexual intercourse for six weeks before a fight. The first man to break the four-minute mile, Roger Bannister, similarly remained celibate before his record-breaking run. The thinking behind this seems to be that sex expends valuable energy that needs to be conserved for the big event. However, sex usually only consumes a low amount of energy – about fifty calories. Scientists have also argued recently that

154

sex before a match or race should actually improve performance: it increases levels of testosterone, which is desirable for competitive events, especially boxing, whereas refraining from sex has the effect of lowering testosterone dramatically.

CHAPTER ELEVEN:
THE WEATHER AND NATURAL OCCURRENCES

'Good Lord...what are the odds on
seeing two strikes in one week ?'

Lightning never strikes twice...

THE WEATHER AND NATURAL OCCURRENCES

'Red sky at night …'
Perhaps one of the best-known old wives' tales states that a red-coloured sky predicts the forthcoming weather:

Red sky at night, shepherd's delight
Red sky in the morning, shepherd's warning.

Oddly enough, this does have some basis in scientific fact. British weather tends to move from west to east, so a sun setting in a clear westerly sky and throwing its glow on to clouds in the east indicates that bad weather had passed over and that the coming conditions are fine. The other way round indicates the opposite situation – that clear weather is soon to be replaced by incoming clouds from the west.

Rain on St Swithin's Day
If it should rain on 15 July, otherwise known as St Swithin's Day, according to the well-known superstition rain will continue for another forty days. The belief reputedly originated in the ninth century when an attempt was made to move the body of St Swithin. Deciding that Winchester Cathedral was a far more fitting resting place than the lowly burial plot that the saint himself had chosen, a group of monks tried to disinter the body, only to find that a rainstorm lasting forty days halted their efforts. The figure of forty days also seems to have a biblical origin, since it was the same amount of rain that prompted Noah to take to his Ark. While this old wives' tale clearly has no basis in science, meteorologists nevertheless do agree that mid-July can be a period of dramatic changes in weather conditions.

Pot of gold at the end of the rainbow

The well-known superstition has it that whoever reaches the mythical rainbow's end will find a pot of gold there. This whimsical idea seems to be of quite recent origin, however, probably popularised by songs and films in the twentieth century, while older beliefs are more inclined to portray the rainbow either as a sign of forthcoming weather or even as an ominous occurrence. Seen in the morning, the rainbow indicates wet weather is on the way, whereas in the evening it is said to forecast dry conditions. At sea, the rainbow is a dreaded sight, since according to sailing folklore it poisoned water by its touch. It also was said to have the ability to suck water from rivers or sea into the clouds, and on occasion would suck up a ship that wandered into its path!

In the Bible, the rainbow may be a sign of God's promise never again to bring a flood upon the world, but in Norse mythology it has quite a different and more sinister significance, and is seen as a 'road of the dead', taking souls from earth to the afterlife. This may be why in some parts of Northern Scotland it is considered a death omen, especially when seen over a house. According to some superstitions it should be 'chased away', so that it takes its bad luck elsewhere. However, it should never be pointed at, since the gesture itself brings bad luck.

Whistling up a gale

At sea, becalmed sailors may fill the sails by whistling as this reputedly raises a wind. They must be very careful when doing this, however, as they may inadvertently whistle up a gale, which is why whistling is usually taboo among sailors. Another method of bringing on the wind is to scratch the mast with a fingernail, or to throw certain objects – coins or a brush – into the sea. In former times it was also common for sailors to purchase wind from a witch in the form of three knots tied into a piece of string. Untying one knot would bring a slight wind, two would produce a stronger wind, and all three would result in a storm. The source of such arcane seagoing superstitions are mysterious but, according to many old wives' tales in coastal districts, witches may influence the weather and were sometimes supposed to set sail in 'egg boats' in order to sink ships (see page 131).

Lightning never strikes twice

The idea that the same place will never be struck twice by lightning is a well-known one, but is unfortunately nonsense. The Empire State Building has been struck over sixty times in a single year, for instance. Many superstitions from the nineteenth century dictate that mirrors, scissors and other reflective surfaces should be covered during a storm since they attract lightning, and that all doors and windows should be opened to allow lightning out should it ender the house. Other safety measures involve staying away from the pet dog, since dogs' tails are reputed to attract lightning!

It is sometimes said that looking directly at lightning may make you insane, but another old wives' tale portrays lightning in more sympathetic terms, claiming that it is created by the Virgin Mary to warn people Satan's thunder is on the way. Perhaps one of the strangest beliefs is that lightning strikes leave behind what are known as the 'Devil's pebbles': stones in the shape of arrowheads that, if collected, may possess magical properties.

Sun on Easter Day

One superstition has it that the sun's rays, if seen reflected in a bucket of water on Easter Sunday, may indicate weather to come. If the reflection is clear and still, fine weather is ahead, but, if the rays appear unstable and broken, bad weather can be expected. The precise origin of this belief is not known, but it is related to many other superstitions about this time of year. Easter Sunday is considered one of the most sacred and auspicious days of the year, when occurrences and behaviour are highly significant and may augur a great deal about the coming season.

If the sun comes out on Candlemas Day there will be two winters

Candlemas, or 2 February, was considered an important day in rural communities. It marked the halfway point between winter and spring, and meant the worst of the year was over and spring could be looked forward to. If, however, spring should start too early, it was a bad sign, and should the sun appear on this day there would be six more weeks of cold weather, or effectively two winters. A variation of the tradition continues today in the American custom of Groundhog Day on which the appearance of a groundhog from its hibernation may indicate when the start of spring will be.

Low-flying swallows

Those wishing to know whether a storm is on the way should watch out for swallows on the wing, since according to a popular old wives' tale their height is an indication of the weather:

Swallows fly high, no rain in the sky,
Swallows fly low, 'tis likely to blow.

Meteorological evidence suggests there may well be some truth in this rhyme, since the sudden changes in atmospheric pressure that precede a rainstorm can affect the ears and thus the behaviour of swallows and other animals with senses more highly tuned than humans. Similar explanations may be advanced for other old wives' tales concerning animal meteorologists. Seagulls are supposed to fly inland when they sense a storm coming, perhaps understandably, and spiders are reputed to spin webs on the ground rather than higher up, presumably to avoid being blown away. It is even conceivable that changes in atmosphere and moisture in the air may result in other supposed harbingers of wet weather – aching corns and rheumatism. Less apparent, however, is the logic behind other old wives' tales stating that the onset of bad weather is predicted by bread falling butter-side down or salt sticking together.

A cat's behaviour foretells the weather

A cat behaving in a mischievous or playful way indicates bad weather to come, according to an eighteenth-century rhyme:

> Against the times of snow or hail,
> Or boist'rous windy storms;
> She frisks about and wags her tail,
> And many tricks performs.

A cat sitting with its back to the fire, meanwhile, is an omen of a sudden change in the weather, and usually frost or a cold spell. Rain is on the way if a cat is seen washing itself: an early sixteenth-century source comments that a cat that puts its feet behind its head to 'lycke hr ars' is a harbinger of wet weather. This perhaps explains why cats feature so prominently in seafaring folklore, since a sudden change in the weather on board a ship could easily mean the death of the crew. According to the superstitions of sailors, however, cats not only foretold but could even control the weather. Trapping a cat was said to raise a storm, and many seafaring wives shut theirs in a cupboard just when they wanted to keep their husbands on shore. In the nineteenth century, Charles Darwin reported that his sailors believed someone on shore had trapped a cat under a tub, preventing them from setting sail. These superstitions were taken so seriously that even the word 'cat' was taboo among Scottish fishermen until well into the twentieth century.

When cows lie down it means rain
This is a commonly repeated belief with no known origin. Variations state that, when cows lift their tails or feed close together, wet weather is imminent. If they graze with their tails hitting a fence, however, a spell of fine weather is on the way.

'Rain, rain, go away'

The popular children's rhyme intended to drive away the rain dates back to the seventeenth century and exists in various forms, the most well-known being 'Rain, rain, go away, come again another day'. In some Celtic societies, measures for either bringing or dispelling rain involved immersing a cross into water, or taking it out again. But perhaps the most bizarre practice involves sending a firstborn child naked into the rain and instructing them to stand on their head!

Despite such efforts to stop the rain, rainwater is held to have special properties, and one superstition claims that money washed in it will be safe from thieves, and that washing a baby in rainwater will make them more intelligent. According to German folklore, a child conceived during a rainstorm will be female, whereas one conceived in dry weather is likely to be a boy.

New Year wind

The direction of the wind at the turn of the year predicts weather to come. At the sound of the New Year chimes, a northerly wind means forthcoming bad weather, a southerly wind indicates fine conditions to come, and an easterly wind is an ominous sign, meaning storms are on the way. A westerly breeze means that someone well known will die, and calm, still conditions are a good omen, meaning contentment in the immediate future.

Comets

Since ancient times comets have been looked on with dread. With their distinctive fiery trails, they were described by early commentators as stars with hair or beards, and were said to augur death, plague, war or some other calamity. The Norman invasion of 1066 was famously presaged by an appearance of Halley's comet, and sightings of a comet were thought to have predicted the downfall of the Roman emperor Nero. Even in the present day they are sometimes still looked on with trepidation, and according to superstition no new ventures should be attempted while one is in the sky.

Shooting stars

Making a wish on seeing a falling or shooting star is a fairly common practice nowadays, but in earlier times they were seen as having a different significance. According to Victorian wisdom, the sight of such a star meant a new baby had come into the world. Earlier still, however, they were an ominous sign, meaning that death or other catastrophe was about to occur.

The full moon

The popular association of werewolves with a full moon is probably attributable to horror films, but the idea that exposure to the full moon can produce odd behaviour is one that can be traced back much further to the classical era. The Latin word for moon, *luna*, is the root of the word 'lunacy', and the belief that the moonlight makes you mad is one that was once very widespread. Young women were thought particularly susceptible to being 'moonstruck' and were discouraged from sleeping with the moon shining in through the window.

Gazing at the full moon was often considered taboo for another reason, however. It was said that the moon should be shown respect and that staring at it, or, even worse, pointing, would attract the attention of evil spirits. In some other versions of this superstition, it is the 'man in the moon' who will be antagonised by being pointed at. Reciting the following old rhyme was intended to dispel any bad effects of seeing the moon, and it is still sometimes said today:

I see the moon and the moon sees me.
God bless the moon and God bless me.

The full moon is also said to have the power to cure warts. Those wishing to rid themselves of a wart should blow on to the affected area under the light of a full moon.

The new moon
According to folklore, the new moon is the most auspicious part of the lunar cycle since it symbolises rebirth and should be shown the utmost deference. According to the book of Numbers, a 'burnt offering' should be made every month to the new moon. The crescent-shaped moon should only be looked at from the left, however, and never be seen over the right shoulder, as this attracts bad fortune. Similarly, it should never be looked at through a pane of glass, but only through an open window.

As a potent sign of growth and fertility, many rituals and superstitions surrounded it. Money should be turned over in the pocket on seeing the new moon, since this would cause the money to 'grow' with it. For the same reason, it was considered a good time to sow seed, and farming practices often involved planting 'by the moon'. The slaughtering of animals should be carried out during the moon's growth, as it was thought to produce more succulent meat, and hair should also be cut at this time, since it resulted in luxurious growth. Attending to things that were not desired to be abundant, however, such as nails and corns, was best kept until the waning of the moon, since it slowed their growth.

The new moon may also help a lover to determine whether their feelings are returned, or else to discover how long they will have to wait to be married. When seen in a refracted form either in water, or through a silk handkerchief, the number of moons corresponded to the number of years they would remain single.

CHAPTER TWELVE:
BIRTH

'Oh! Sorry madam...must be a
clerical error.'

Cross dressing can fool the devil...

BIRTH

Easing the pain of childbirth

Just as at the time of a person's death, it was considered very important to untie all knots in the room where a woman was delivering a baby and to open all the windows so as to make the delivery easier. Knots were considered magical in the past since they were thought to hold back spirits and forces, and perhaps they were untied during deliveries as a symbol of release, a fundamental component of any delivery. Various amulets and talismans would be brought to the mother-to-be at the time of delivery: silver coins would be placed in her bed sheets, empty hornets' nests would be left on the table next to her and salt would be placed in her hand. In Ireland it was thought that borrowing a piece of clothing from a cuckolded man and hanging it over the bed would also make the delivery easier, though it is unclear why that should have an effect. Perhaps it was a reminder to the suffering woman that there are worse things in life, or perhaps symbolically summoning up the energy and anger of the cuckolded man was supposed to give the mother strength to push – but these are only speculations. It was considered very lucky for a mother to lie with her head facing north, as this would bring the baby into the world from the south, in the exact alignment of how a person would come out of a church. All of these beliefs existed way before the modern miracle that is the epidural!

Good and bad times to be born

There are various superstitions surrounding one's day of birth. Children born on a Sunday were usually considered blessed, immune from witchcraft and certain never to die by hanging or drowning. It was considered lucky to be born on Christmas Day or New Year's Day, although one superstition suggested that a baby born on

Christmas Day would only live to reach the age of Christ at the time of his crucifixion: thirty-three years, not a very lucky time to die! Babies born on Halloween were thought to have the gift of communicating with the dead (this belief probably stems from Halloween's link to the day of the dead). Children born on the 'chime hours' – meaning three, six, nine and twelve – were thought to be unlucky, although they were also attributed special psychic powers, such as the ability to perceive the unseen and communicate with spirits. Babies born during the day were considered luckier than those born in the middle of the night, and babies born at sunset were said to grow to be lazy as adults. Babies born when the moon is new were thought to be destined to a life of failure or, in other versions of the superstition, to grow to be particularly strong. The most unlucky day of the year to be born was 28 December, possibly due to it being one of the darkest and coldest days of the year.

Today, superstitions surrounding the day of birth have survived only in the form of the children's nursery rhyme:

Monday's child is fair of face,
Tuesday's child is full of grace,
Wednesday's child is full of woe,
Thursday's child has far to go.
Friday's child is loving and giving,
Saturday's child works hard for a living,
But the child born on the Sabbath Day,
Is fair and wise and good and gay.

These beliefs were probably based on now quite obscure ancient superstitions about auspicious and inauspicious days to begin new ventures, which survived into modern times.

Babies born with the caul on their heads
In many countries it was considered lucky to be born with the caul, a thin membrane sometimes found on the baby's head at birth, a remnant of the amniotic sac. In Italy babies born with the caul are said to have been 'born with a shirt', and this has become a common expression there to denote a person with exceptional luck. Being born with the caul supposedly ensured protection against evil forces for the baby's entire life. Babies born with the caul were also thought to have special

psychic powers. The caul would be kept for life and there were various superstitions surrounding it: if it was lost, this was considered ominous for its owner who was to know its whereabouts at all times so as to be sure to be buried with it. Those born with the caul who failed to be buried with it were thought to remain on earth as ghosts, endlessly looking for their lost caul. Cauls were thought to bring good luck not only to those born with it but to anyone possessing one. They were often used as amulets against drowning and shipwrecks, so they were especially sought after by sailors and bought and sold at very high prices, especially in the nineteenth century. The origins of the belief that the caul would protect from drowning can be linked to the fact that babies are able to live and float nicely in the amniotic sac without drowning.

Washing, grooming and dressing a baby
There were many dangers associated with washing and dressing a baby. It was common practice not to wash a baby's right hand for the first three days of its life because this was thought to wash away its luck. Especially after a baby's first

bath, but for most baths subsequently, the water would have to be carefully poured over a tree in leaf to help the child grow healthy. If the water was poured over a tree at the time of flowering, it was considered particularly good for the child who would grow to be exceptionally beautiful. When babies were dressed for the first time it was important that they were dressed only in used clothes, as new clothes would attract evil spirits and witches. It was always customary to start dressing a baby from its feet rather than from its head. It was considered very unlucky to cut a baby's hair before it had turned one, or for a mother to cut a baby's nails with scissors in the first year of its life. Biting nails off was the recommended method instead. This superstition probably simply originated in the very practical fact that babies' nails are extremely delicate and small and that it is much safer and easier for a mother to feel the nails in her mouth than to try to use a tool. Furthermore, scissors were often made of iron, which was considered a very powerful metal that could protect against witches but could also expose an infant to excessively dangerous forces.

Cross-dressing confuses the Devil

It was common, until the latter half of the nineteenth century and even as late as the early part of the twentieth century, to dress little boys in girls' clothes and to let them grow beautiful long curls so as to confuse the Devil and avert the evil eye. This bizarre practice was linked to the misogynous belief that girls were inferior to boys and that they were thus less likely to be attacked by demons and witches. Indeed, it was because boys were considered at much higher risk of being snatched by demons, witches and fairies that they were usually dressed in blue – the colour of the Virgin Mary. The practice of dressing little girls in pink is much more recent and does not seem to have any particular superstitious meaning behind it. Dressing children in black was considered very unlucky since black was traditionally considered the colour of death and would thus expose the child to the risk of an early death (quite common before the twentieth century). Even today it is difficult to find an entirely black child's garment in children's boutiques, although we no longer live by such fearful superstitions concerning colours.

Protecting unbaptised babies from danger

The time between a baby's birth and its baptism was considered a most dangerous time, when they could be snatched away by witches and fairies, be replaced by a changeling or die an early death. Babies who died before being baptised were traditionally thought to end up in limbo, a part of hell where they would languish away from the light of God and in misery for all eternity. In Scandinavia, babies who died before being baptised were thought to transform into the dim lights that are sometimes visible over marshy fields, known as the 'will-o'-the-wisps', and forever haunt the earth in clusters of wailing babies.

High early infant mortality rates, bad hygiene and poor nutrition for mothers in the past can explain the sense of anxiety surrounding the early days of a newborn baby and the multiple superstitions concerning its protection. It was common to wrap an infant in clothes belonging to its parents, especially the mother because it was thought that contact with an extension of the mother's body would protect the child. It was considered very unlucky to compliment a child because this could attract the envy of witches and evil spirits (this belief is still common today in China where babies are greeted with insults rather than compliments and proud parents simply have to reverse the insults in their minds). Babies were often welcomed into the world by being spat at three times as protection against evil spirits. Silver or iron amulets and communion wafers were once placed in a baby's crib and sometimes a knife was tied to the crib as well as a red string, a traditional protection against witches. Until the baby was baptised, it was important for all visitors to the household to make a toast and to eat something to protect the health of the child. It was also thought that, if a baby saw his reflection in the mirror before being baptised, he would die instantly and various precautions were taken to prevent such an occurrence from happening.

The changeling

The superstition surrounding the changeling is one of the most horrific and heart-breaking of old beliefs and superstitious practices. It was thought that fairies, envious of a human child's natural beauty and health, would sometimes kidnap it and replace it with their own monstrous baby. This changeling was a misshapen baby, sometimes hairy, thought to eat enormous amounts of food, never to grow and to cry continuously. If parents suddenly noticed a severe handicap in their child, such as when a child was hydrocephalic or had Down's Syndrome, or if it was experiencing deformities and stunted growth due to malnutrition, they would explain it to themselves and others by suggesting that their real child had been kidnapped and replaced by a monster. The shocking part of this belief is that, in order to see if a baby was a true changeling, it would be exposed to several trials that would often result in the death of the baby: disabled babies would be placed near a roaring fire, and if they were real changelings they were thought to climb up the chimney to escape (probably a euphemism for being burned alive). Other ways of checking to see if a baby was a true changeling included making the baby sleep outdoors, often in the dead of winter, and checking if it managed to survive the night, or repeatedly whipping it to see if it would utter horrible screams. Needless to say, these beliefs no longer survive in our society, and we can only be thankful that our understanding of genetics and modern medicine have cured us of such cruel barbarisms and taught us to treat children suffering from such disorders with love and care instead.

Baptism and naming rituals

The Christian ritual of baptism introduces a child into the life of the Church and cleanses it of original sin. Baptism has its roots in much earlier pagan naming rituals. During baptism children are given their Christian names and in the past it was common for this name to be chosen from the pages of lives of the saints, according to the specific date of their baptism. Thus, very unpopular names were accepted by often reluctant parents, who nevertheless felt that their baby was being protected by the saint corresponding to their baptism day.

It was considered lucky for a child to cry during the baptism ceremony, especially at the time of receiving the holy water on their heads, as this was meant to be a sign that evil forces were exiting the baby's body and that it was being successfully purified. It was important for the child to be dressed entirely in white and it was considered best if the baptism gown was not brand new but had been used before, so as not to attract the evil eye. It was thought that wetting the eyes of the baby with holy water would protect it from seeing the apparitions of the dead later in life. It was also generally advised to let the holy water dry naturally on the baby's head and not to dry it so as to allow it fully to permeate the little one's body. It was considered unlucky for a baptism to occur in a church straight after a funeral, and even more unlucky for a baptismal party to run into a funeral procession or a cemetery. Baptismal processions would therefore be very careful to avoid the graveyard when entering the church. By contrast, baptisms held right after weddings were considered very lucky.

There are many superstitions surrounding names, and the belief that knowing a person's full name gave one power probably originated in Roman times, when Romans would find out the name of the patron deity of an enemy city and then perform rituals and offerings to those gods so that they would transfer their power and protection to Rome instead. Nicknames given to children were thus not only used for brevity and practical purposes, but also to protect the child's full name from being called out by evil forces. It was thought that speaking a person's name would summon them, and the expression 'speak of the Devil, tread on its tail' emerged from that superstition.

Birthstones

Although they reached the apex of their commercial success in recent years, birthstones can be linked back to Exodus 28:15–21. Moses commanded his brother Aaron to fabricate a breastplate covered in precious stones made of twelve different colours to represent the twelve tribes of Israel. A specific stone was then chosen to correspond to each colour and was later linked to the months of the year. The number twelve has a deep religious resonance in Western culture since it is the number not only of the tribes of Israel, but also of the Apostles, the months of the year and the signs of the zodiac. Gemstones in general were attributed various powers by superstition, and birthstones would heighten the supposed power of the gems for those born in the months corresponding to them. Here is a list of the most commonly known meanings of birthstones and of some of the properties attributed to these gems in the past.

January: Garnet

The word 'garnet' derives from the word 'pomegranate', which has the same colour as the stone. Because in its most precious form the stone has a particular red colour, considered sacred and chosen for religious rituals, it is a stone denoting faith, constancy and truth. It is also said to have healing powers. As a talisman the garnet is meant to provide protection for travellers, especially against disease. It is also supposed to protect against mental instability, getting wounded in battle and snakebites. It is common to give garnets in jewellery to celebrate a couple's second wedding anniversary. This may be a way of marking the true beginning of the marriage, after the initial 'honeymoon' is over.

February: Amethyst

The word 'amethyst' means 'not intoxicated' and the stone was used as a talisman and sometimes embedded in cups to help prevent intoxication from alcohol. The name for the stone came from an Ancient Greek myth concerning the god of wine Dionysus (Bacchus in the Roman form) and the beautiful moon goddess Artemis (Diana to the Romans). Dionysus, an ugly faun-like god, had tried to seduce Artemis, and when she refused him he became terribly angry and vowed to have tigers devour anyone who entered the moon goddess's forest. The nymph Amethyst was the first to enter the forest to worship Artemis, and when she saw the tigers approaching her she begged her goddess to save her. Artemis immediately turned Amethyst into a white stone, and when Dionysus saw what had happened to the pious nymph he became repentant and poured wine over her stone to apologise. The stone immediately turned the purple violet colour for which it is best known. According to superstition, amethysts are supposed to help intelligence, to protect from the evils of drink and to guard against evil thoughts. It is traditionally seen to give men sound judgement and to strengthen religious love in women and to help them reach high levels of transcendence and enlightenment.

March: Aquamarine

The name aquamarine literally means 'sea water' and comes from its particular blue-green colour. In the Middle Ages, it was supposed to be a stone that would help soothsayers see into the future. It was also thought to help against insomnia as well as being used as a talisman for ocean travellers. For those born in March it is supposed to signify happiness and everlasting youth.

April: Diamond

Diamonds are considered lucky because they are so rare. As symbols of marital love, thought to bring courage to men and to inspire pride in women, they are the traditional stones chosen for engagement rings. Diamonds that reveal bright colours inside them are considered especially lucky and anticipate a particularly prosperous marriage. Diamonds in talismans were thought to protect against poison, fears, nightmares, possession by the Devil and the power of witches. For those born in April, the diamond is supposed to bring power, success, everlasting youth and happiness. Diamonds were sometimes used to determine a wife's faithfulness, with various tests including placing a diamond on her naked breast at night to see if its colour changed, or placing it on her forehead to see in which direction she turned her head. If the diamond became dim, or if she turned her face away from her spouse, this was supposed to be a sign of infidelity.

May: Emerald

Emeralds traditionally signified kindness, faith and the bounty of nature. Their green colour linked them to the colour of new leaves in the spring; they became symbols of new life and were considered particularly effective in curing diseases – epilepsy and high fever in particular. For those born in the month of May, emeralds are meant to bring love and success.

June: Pearl

Pearls are associated with tears, and because of their marine origin they are considered dangerous and thus potentially unlucky, especially for brides, who risk having a marriage full of tears if they wear pearls on their wedding day. The sea origin of pearls linked them in ancient times to the goddess of love Venus, who was famously born in the sea. Pearls were also linked to the moon goddess Diana, however, and were thus lucky gems for hunters who worshipped the goddess. Partially because of its link to Diana, the pearl is seen as the gem of modesty and purity. They are supposed to strengthen friendships, bring solace in difficult times and strengthen memories, as well as being seen to cure blood disorders and fight pestilence.

July: Ruby

Rubies were particularly cherished in India where they were thought to bring a life of peace, tranquillity and good health to those who owned them. In the late seventeenth century, they were often crushed into potions to prevent and cure various diseases. Some thought rubies were good for the brain, for memory and for the heart, and they were particularly prized as blood purifiers. Because of their red colour, which associated them with anger, they were thought to help handle fits of rage and to bring reconciliation to warring parties. As the birthstone for the month of July they signify contentment.

August: Peridot

Peridots are known as the gems of the sun because of their brightness. Just like bright candles, they were traditionally thought capable of chasing away evil spirits as well as the dark and terrifying forces of the night, including nightmares. They were also thought to bring mental stability, kindness and oratory skill. Placed under a person's tongue, they were supposed to help fight the dryness of the mouth due to fever. They were used in talismans but were supposedly most effective if set in gold. Some sources say that a particularly powerful talisman against evil spirits was made by tying a peridot to one's left arm using a string made from the hair of a donkey. When ground into powder, peridots were thought to be efficient medicine against asthma. As August's birthstone, peridots signify married happiness.

September: Sapphire

In the book of Revelation, sapphires are mentioned as the second stone in the foundation of the new Jerusalem and are thus considered particularly sacred, thought to attract the favour of God. Sapphires were believed to bring good luck to their owners and to ward off evil spirits. It was also thought that reptiles and insects would die immediately if they came in contact with the stone. Sapphires are supposed to bring wisdom and clarity of mind to those born in September.

October: Opal

The word opal comes from the Latin *opulus* and the Sanskrit *upala* – both of which mean 'precious stone'. Traditionally, the opal is considered the unluckiest of all precious stones and only those born in October are thought to be allowed to wear it safely. It is thought that engagement rings made of such a stone suggest that the bride shall be a widow early in the marriage. If a diamond is present together with the opal, however, the diamond's strong positive powers are thought to counter any bad luck contained in the opal stone. Black opals, though, are considered lucky. The bad luck associated with opals may be connected to their changeable nature – they reflect different colours according to their environment – which was seen as being the work of witchcraft. Another possible reason may be the stone's brittle nature, which would often result in broken jewels, surely a sign of bad luck.

Conversely, opals were seen as a gem of inspiration in the arts and in love. It was thought they could make their owners invisible to enemies, and they were also believed to be useful in talismans against evil thoughts, kidney disease and cholera. In Ancient Rome opals were symbols of hope and purity, and in Ancient Greece they gave their owners the gift of prophecy. Another popular superstition surrounding opals is that they help preserve the gold in blond hair. The meaning of the opal birthstone is hope.

November: Topaz
The name topaz is derived from the Sanskrit *topas*, which means 'fire'. Used in amulets, topaz stones are thought to protect against sadness, to give courage and to give the mind strength. Mounted in gold and kept around the neck, topaz stones were thought to be magical remedies against enchantment. Perhaps because of its association with fire, the stone was meant to help calm passions. It was also used as a remedy against bad dreams and it was thought to help achieve a peaceful death, free from fear. Because it was often associated with St Mathew, the topaz was seen to

symbolise faith and charity, true friendship, everlasting love, beauty and wisdom. Its birthstone meaning is fidelity.

December: Turquoise

The name turquoise comes from the Old French turquoise, meaning 'Turkish', presumably because of the geographic origin of the stone. Turquoise stones were thought to be particularly effective in fighting the evil eye and were worn by Native Americans. During the Middle Ages, in Europe they were used to protect citizens from the plague, and they were also used in talismans to protect travellers. They are thought to be the stone of self-realisation and to help in analytical thinking. They are also similar to amethysts in the sense that they are thought to absorb negativity and protect against intoxication and poison. Their meaning for those born in December is creativity, wholeness and emotional balance.

CHAPTER THIRTEEN:
DEATH

Never speak ill of the dead!

DEATH

A good death

There are many superstitions concerning the ways to help loved ones have a 'good' death, easing their physical pain and helping them into the afterlife. A commonly held superstition was connected to the positioning of the bed of a dying man in relation to the floorboards: it was supposedly easier for a person to die if the bed was lined up in the same direction. It was also important that nobody stood at the foot of the bed so as not to block the departing soul's passage into the afterlife. For a similar reason the doors and windows in a dead person's room were to be kept wide open. Knots were also thought to hinder a soul's safe passage to the afterlife, so it was important to untie all knots in a dying person's room. These beliefs are known to date back at least as far as the sixteenth century, but are probably even older.

Mirrors were also thought to hold the soul of the dead person back in the house, and they were often covered to help the dead leave this world safely. In some countries this practice extended to all shiny objects where a reflection could be seen. This superstition may be linked to ancient superstitions concerning reflections (see the entry on breaking a mirror on page 35). It could also be linked to the sense that reflections capture something of the soul of those looking into them. If the dying person was captured in the mirror, a part of his soul would forever linger in the house. Finally, there is a deeply ingrained superstition concerning the proper way of taking a corpse out of a house, to ensure that it will have a good departure from this life. In a direct reversal to the way it came into this world, a dead body is supposed to exit the house feet first and the doors to the house must not be closed until the final funeral guest has left the house.

Good days of the year to die

A person who dies on Good Friday goes straight to heaven: to die on the same day that Christ died was considered blessed. To die at midnight on Christmas Eve would also ensure immediate ascension to heaven because it was thought that at that time the gates of heaven would open each year.

Speaking ill of the dead

It is considered unlucky and dangerous to speak ill of the dead. This belief dates back to Roman times and perhaps even earlier. Measures to prevent untoward things from happening due to bad-mouthing the departed are still taken today. It was thought that to speak badly of the dead would disturb dead souls in their eternal sleep and might accidentally summon them up for an unwanted and unexpected visit. It was to stop such an occurrence from taking place that conventional phrases such as 'May God bless his soul!' or 'May she rest in peace!' became common and are still widely spoken today. Other expressions such as adding 'poor soul' or simply adding 'poor' to the deceased's name are also common.

Touching a corpse brings luck

To touch a corpse is considered lucky and is supposed to help the newly departed rest in peace. In some accounts the practice is thought to protect the living from dreaming of, or being haunted by, the ghost of the deceased. The practice of ritually touching the corpse during a viewing is very old, appearing for example in medieval sagas such as the *Nibelungenlied* (immortalised by Richard Wagner's *Ring* cycle). A medieval superstition that was still commonly believed (and used as evidence in courts of law) as late as the seventeenth century held that if the corpse of a murdered person was touched by its murderer it would start bleeding a second time, denouncing and condemning its killer.

Death omens

If a corpse remains warm and soft for a longer time than is normally expected, this is supposed to be a terrible omen, predicting that a death in the corpse's family will occur soon. In the past it was also considered bad luck for a person to die with his or her eyes open, as this was also thought to bring a second death in the household since the corpse was thought to be looking for death's next victim. This belief may be at the origins of our contemporary habit of closing the eyes of the departed after death (although it is more likely associated with our discomfort at seeing familiar eyes, usually full of expression, stare back at us in lifeless form).

Sailors believe that to look at the coffin of a person that has died at sea as it is thrown into the waves brings bad luck. He who looks at the coffin as it reaches the water is sure to die soon.

If a wedding ring is accidentally dropped by a spouse during the wedding ceremony, he or she will be the first in the couple to die. If the ring is dropped by a third party and rolls on to a gravestone in the church this is a death omen, announcing the impending death of the bride or groom according to the gender of the person interred under the gravestone.

Another more well-known death omen is related to portraits and photographs. If a picture suddenly falls off the wall and breaks, it is considered a death omen for the person depicted in the picture or for somebody in their family. The origins of this belief can be traced back at least to the late seventeenth century, but this superstition became much more common with the spread of personal photography at the end of the nineteenth century, and is often used as a narrative device in films.

Suicides

Because of the very strict religious prohibition against the act of committing suicide, there are many dark beliefs surrounding the bodies and souls of those who take their own life. One very commonly held tradition is that the spirit of suicides haunts the places where their death occurred. In the past the bodies of suicides were buried outside of sacred ground or in the northern part of the graveyard, the most unlucky part of the graveyard where the bodies of fallen women, unclaimed corpses, unbaptised children and criminals were also buried. They would not receive religious rites and this was also at the root of why suicides were thought to remain on earth in the form of ghosts. Before a law against it was passed in the early nineteenth century, suicides were often buried at crossroads so as to confuse the suicide's ghost and make it difficult for it to return to the town or city to haunt it. For similar reasons, a wooden stake was often used to pierce the heart of the dead so as to keep their body and soul immobilised and pinned to the ground – it wasn't until the early nineteenth century that a law was passed against this barbaric practice. Suicides were only officially granted religious rites in 1882, but there remained a widely held belief that the bodies of suicides would not start to decay until the date of their God-intended natural death was reached.

Funerals

It is considered unlucky to meet a funeral head on. To avoid the bad luck associated with such an event people are encouraged to join the funeral cortege briefly, so that one is then leaving rather than meeting it. It is also considered bad luck to point at a funeral procession (probably due to the superstition around pointing – see page 29). The funeral procession, according to tradition, must never be interrupted or this might cause the ghost of the recently departed to slip away and return to haunt the living. Another version of the same superstition suggests that to interrupt the funeral procession would bring bad luck in the form of a new death in the family shortly thereafter. It was also considered unlucky to glance at a funeral procession through a window or, worse still, through a mirror, as that too would announce an imminent death. The custom of wearing black when mourning, beside connoting the lack of joy in a person's life once a loved one has passed away, seems to have originated in the belief that the Devil could not see black and that, since he would be around at a person's funeral looking for souls to kidnap, to wear black would protect the mourners from being snatched away. Giving food to friends and relatives attending the funeral was thought to bring good luck to all those attending, as well as being a sign of respect and thanks to the departed. It was considered unlucky and was absolutely discouraged for a pregnant woman to attend a funeral. This was probably because of the taboo of mixing together a new life and a new death, as well as the fear that the spirit of the dead might come back in the form of the newborn baby.

Sin eaters

Starting in the Middle Ages, a peculiar custom began to accompany funeral celebrations: the hiring of a sin eater. It was believed that, if people ate food that had come into contact with or had at least been in close proximity to the corpse, the dead person's sins would be transferred to them and the dead would reach heaven faster. Few people would obviously volunteer for such an activity as it would bring sins upon them, so it was therefore common practice to hire professional sin eaters, mostly chosen from the starving poor, to consume the sins of the dead. The practice has been abandoned in the modern age, but reminders of it can be found in some funeral traditions such as the drinking of beer from glasses placed on a dead man's coffin. In such customs it is considered ill-mannered and unlucky not to drink from such glasses, as this is showing disrespect to the dead, and indirectly an unwillingness to drink their sins. The habit of serving food at wakes and funerals may also be a remnant of this medieval superstition.

CHAPTER FOURTEEN:
NUMBERS, LUCKY AND UNLUCKY

Unlucky 13

NUMBERS

In general in Europe and the Middle East world, odd numbers were attributed special powers and meaning, while most even numbers were considered neutral and not very useful in magic and superstition. Below are the most 'powerful' numbers, which recurred often in rituals or had special lucky or unlucky meanings.

One

The number one was used to represent God. It was attributed great importance since it is the fundamental unit making up all other numbers: indivisible and all powerful. It was and still is considered lucky to live in a house whose street number is one, and it is also considered very lucky to be born on the first day of the month. In China, however, the word for the number one resembles the sound of the word for 'loneliness', so it is considered unlucky.

Three

The number three is one of the most powerful numbers, recurring in very many religions across the world. The Ancient Greeks, and in particular Pythagoras and his followers, thought it was the most perfect number since it contained within it everything: the beginning, the middle and the end of all things. It was the Pythagoreans who first began to see magic in the equilateral triangle, and this symbol was used in magic rituals for centuries to come, seen as embodying the special power of three. The equilateral triangle also figures prominently in the iconography of Masonic secret societies, where it is sometimes shown with an eye in the middle, as appears in the US dollar bill – much to the delight of conspiracy theorists. Two equilateral triangles placed adjacent to each other were often used in rituals aimed at fighting evil forces.

Christians took the special meaning of the number three in their conceptualisation of the Holy Trinity of Father, Son and Holy Spirit. The Trinity is not unique to Christianity: it is also present in Hinduism (in the *Trimurti* – the Trinity of Brahma, Vishnu and Shiva), in Buddhism (where the Buddha appears in three forms) as well as in many African societies and ancient Latin American societies where the Trinity often appeared in the shape of father, mother and son.

Following the special powers of the number three, popular superstition sees both positive and negative things happening 'in threes'. Breaking things around the house was thought to happen in threes, so especially in the nineteenth century it became common to break two less valuable objects following a breakage in the household, to prevent other more valuable things from being damaged. Three candles burning in a room were seen as omens of death, as were three distinct knocks heard in the room of a dying man or woman. It was thought that deaths and accidents would come in threes. A much earlier superstition, dating back to the fourteenth century, suggested that the third time is lucky when people attempted things unsuccessfully, or played games. In rituals, gestures were often repeated three times: spitting three times was thought to ward off evil, and many treatments in folk medicine were to be taken three times, or in multiples of three, to ensure a rapid cure.

Four

Although it is an even number, the number four was also considered holy by those involved in numerology and mysticism. For Christians the number four is sacred because of the four gospels. In the Jewish tradition the number four corresponded to the Tetragrammaton, the four-letter word denoting God, which was considered so sacred that it was never spoken out loud – although it appears in the Hebrew Bible 6,823 times. In China and Japan the number four is considered unlucky because it resembles the sound of the word 'death' in both languages. Hospitals therefore never have a fourth floor, and most people try to avoid licence plates with that number or house numbers bearing the number four on them.

Five

Five was considered a magic number in many places and by various civilisations. From the Maya to the Ancient Egyptians to the Pythagorean Greeks, five was seen as a powerful number. The five-pointed star was a universally revered symbol and for the Pythagoreans as it represented light. The pentagram – a five-pointed star with a pentagon in the middle – was used as a deterrent against evil forces and spirits. In the past it was a symbol of knowledge and wisdom. In its upside-down form the pentagram is a symbol of evil and of the Devil (the two points suggesting the Devil's horns), and it is now often used in films to denote black magic and satanic rituals.

Seven

In the ancient (and later the medieval) world, there were thought to be seven planets including the sun and the moon, seven phases of the moon, seven metals, seven ages of man, seven deadly sins, seven graces and seven virtues. God created the earth and all its creatures in six days and the seventh day was a day of rest, so particularly sacred. The number seven also corresponded to twice the number three and the number one, which made it a particularly holy number, as did the fact that it was indivisible. In Christianity there are seven sacraments.

There are many superstitions surrounding the number seven. If one's date of birth can be turned into a number that is divisible by seven, one will lead an exceptionally happy life. Breaking a mirror brings seven years of bad luck. It is particularly unlucky to get married on 7 April or 7 December. The seventh child of a seventh child will have psychic powers. An infertile woman can become pregnant if she wraps her husband's belt seven times around a tree. To wash one's hair on the seventh day of the lunar cycle brings problems with the law to one's home. To dream about the number seven is an omen that one is about to meet one's future husband or wife.

Eight
In China, eight is the luckiest number of all because the sound of the word 'eight' in Chinese is very similar to the word for 'lucky'. There are several western superstitions surrounding this number, and their origins are mostly obscure. It

is said to be unlucky to give a friend or a loved one a bouquet made up of eight flowers. Washing one's hair on the eighth of the month ensures that one will reach a ripe old age. To dream of the number eight is a sign that one is about to lose money.

Nine

The number nine was considered particularly powerful, and many rituals and spells called for things to be repeated nine times. The number nine is composed of three times the number three and it also corresponds to the number of months in the human gestation period. Nine was sacred to the Norse. There are various superstitions involving the number nine. It is lucky to find nine peas in a pod. Tying nine knots in a loved one's hair will bring them to you. To live in a house whose street number is nine causes longevity. A young man who wishes to marry should count ninety-nine stars in the sky for nine consecutive days and he will find a wife. It is extremely unlucky to find the card representing the nine of diamonds on the street. Washing one's hair on the ninth day of the month brings a happy marriage.

A cat is thought to have nine lives. Getting married on 9 December is unlucky. To dream of the number nine is a sign that a child is on its way.

Thirteen

The number thirteen is often considered unlucky because there were thirteen people at the Last Supper. Superstition has it that it is very unlucky to have a dinner party with thirteen guests. Many hotels do not have rooms with the number thirteen, and many tall buildings don't have a thirteenth floor. It is supposedly unlucky to live in a house whose street number is thirteen. Friday the thirteenth is considered an extremely unlucky day, but this belief only dates back to the nineteenth century and belongs mostly to the British Isles and North America – in southern Europe it is Friday the seventeenth that is considered unlucky instead. Friday is the day that Christ was crucified, which explains the superstitions that arose around that day of the week. Washing one's hair on the thirteenth of the month will bring a male child, and the thirteenth card in the major arcana of the tarot deck is the card for death.

666

According to Revelation 13:16–18, 666 is the 'number of the beast'. The famous fire of 1666 in London gave the number of the beast a particularly frightening resonance.

CHAPTER FIFTEEN:
GIFTS

Giving knives as gifts can have
terrible consequences…

GIFTS

Giving sharp objects, especially knives or scissors

One should never give sharp objects such as knives or scissors to a friend without taking the necessary countermeasures. In order to avoid a curse being put upon them, the friend must give something back to the giver, a symbolic sum of money or perhaps a bit of salt. The symbolic return gift ensures that the objects appear to have been purchased rather than given and thus the 'curse' on the friendship is lifted. Knives and scissors, in fact, are seen to cut the bonds of love or luck running between the two friends. Giving a luck penny or a small coin is also practised in ribbon-cutting ceremonies to make up for the potentially malicious gesture of passing a sharp object to another person. These superstitions hark back at least to the sixteenth century in Britain. In the past scissors were seen to be lucky objects and were thought to scare away witches and to have special powers since they are made of metal. Some sources claim that it was common to place scissors under the doormat in order to keep witches out of the house, so giving scissors (with the necessary countermeasure) could be seen to bring protection to the household and to keep evil forces out.

Giving bouquets of red and white flowers

It is considered very unlucky for a bouquet to be made up of red and white flowers as this is an omen of death. The spell is apparently dissolved if even just one or two flowers of a different colour are included in the bouquet. In hospitals, however, it is highly inappropriate for the two flowers to appear together at all. One commonly touted explanation is that the red and white colours are reminiscent of blood and bandages and thus unlucky in the home and in the hospital.

Another explanation is that white and red are the colours of milk and blood, two very powerful bodily fluids associated with birth and death respectively. References to this superstition, however, are relatively recent, dating back to the late nineteenth century, and may simply be attributed to the Victorian meanings given to flowers and colours: white was considered unlucky and suitable for a funeral; red represented anger and powerful forces (sometimes passion, but in this case blood and death).

Amber beads

A superstitious remedy against sickness was to wear a necklace made of amber beads. Amber beads were thought to fight colds, whooping cough, asthma and nasal congestion. They were also thought to evoke sympathy and compassion for those who wore them, so they are an ideal present for a friend who is often sick.

Gifts for a new bride and a new home

It is unlucky to pay a visit to a new household without a present and it is recommended to bring a small object that may be of use in the new house, or something living such as a potted plant bearing flowers. It is considered particularly lucky to give a couple starting a new home rough salt. This custom probably originates from a time when salt was particularly expensive and used in large amounts for preserving food as well as for protection against evil spirits and witches. As with most new beginnings, starting a new home was considered a dangerous activity, attracting the envy and rage of witches, and a newlywed couple would thus need protection from those dear to them. It is considered very lucky to give a bride a wooden spoon as it is meant to help her get pregnant quickly. The origins of this superstition, like many similar superstitions linking spoons with children and fertility, do not seem to date back much earlier than Victorian times when spoons were linked with sexual innuendo especially due to the way they are stacked together (as in the expression 'spooning'). Spoons were also probably seen to be symbolic equivalents of a woman's pregnant form due to their rounded shape. There is also a superstition about giving a new broomstick to a female friend when visiting a new home. This is in order to wipe the new home clean of any pre-existing bad spirits

and energies and also to regenerate female power –
in the past only associated with the household (and
behind the imagery of witches flying on
broomsticks as symbols of domestic power that
runs amok in popular lore).

Gifts for friends

In spite of the contemporary popularity of giving
bath salts and soaps to friends, an old superstition
guarded against giving soap to a friend as this was
supposed to 'wash away' the friendship. Similarly,
it was considered very unlucky to give a friend an
umbrella as this would bring rain to the friendship
(this superstition can only be seen to date back to
the beginning of the nineteenth century for the
obvious reason that umbrellas were scarcely used
before then). Clocks in general have been
associated with death so it is considered unlucky
to give a clock or a watch to a friend. The origins
of this superstition date back to when clocks were
mechanical and needed to be wound by hand. If a
person was sick it was very likely that they would
forget to wind their own watch or the household
clock, so a watch or clock would be found stopped
when a person died.

Gifts at the theatre

It is considered unlucky to give flowers to an actor or actress before the performance as this is seen as tempting fate – as an act of excessive confidence it is thought to doom their performance. On the other hand, it is very lucky to receive flowers in the dressing room after the performance, especially roses. To wear blue or yellow during a performance is thought to make actors forget their lines; by extension giving actors anything blue or yellow before the performance is not recommended. Because actors were traditionally thought to be very superstitious, to give them any kind of amulet or talisman, especially one that could be easily worn under a costume, is a perfect gift.

Gifts for a newborn baby at his or her baptism

At a baby's baptism the most important figures are traditionally the godparents, who are expected to provide the nicest and most lavish gifts for the child. Starting in the fifteenth century it became customary for godparents to give silver spoons or cups to the baby. Silver was considered a very powerful metal that brought luck and could protect its bearer from enchantment. The expression 'to be born with a silver spoon in the mouth' is a way of saying that a person has been blessed since birth, originally implying that they had rich godparents who could provide expensive gifts. Other traditional gifts, meant to provide the baby with protection against witches, were jewels made of coral. Today it is still common to give gifts of silver, even though their protective quality against witches has long been forgotten.

CHAPTER SIXTEEN:
CELEBRATIONS AND FESTIVALS

'Blasted bachelors have been at
the cabbages again.'

Unmarried men can see what their
future wives will look like in pulled up
cabbage stalks!

CELEBRATIONS AND FESTIVALS

The first person seen on New Year's Day should be male

Take care that the first person you meet on 1 January is a man. The custom of 'first-footing' dictates that the gender of the person encountered immediately after midnight on New Year's Eve carries great significance. It is very unlucky if it happens to be a woman. If the person is a man, especially one who is both tall and dark, this betokens good luck for the year to come. Since the nineteenth century, this superstition has been found in many parts of Britain, but is especially well known in Scotland. Some local variations demand that not only must this 'first-footer' be male, but also a particular kind of person with flat feet and eyebrows that meet in the middle; meanness and blindness are considered unlucky features, as are men with professions such as doctor and vicar. Thieves and those armed with a knife are similarly inauspicious. Unsurprisingly, it is common to arrange a visit from a desirable first-footer rather than leave their identity to chance. Accordingly, the man in question should enter a house shortly after the turn of the year, ideally carrying a coin, a piece of bread and a coal to symbolise prosperity for the coming year. He will wish everyone present a happy new year, stoke the fire and enter every room in the house in turn. Often he is required to enter through the front door and exit though the back.

Fires must be kept burning on New Year's Eve
Don't let the fire in the hearth go out before the morning of 1 January. According to old wives' tales, circumstances on this night will affect fortunes for the next twelve months and the fire, as heart of the household, should be treated with special reverence. Lit coals should not be taken

away from a hearth for the same reason. Related superstitions dictate that new clothes should be worn on New Year's morning, and that getting up early on this day meant an industrious and productive year. It is unwise to lend out money or belongings and, while things may be brought into a house at this time, on no account must items be taken out. In some cases, this meant keeping hold of household waste until the New Year had properly begun, in order that the period ahead should be a prosperous one.

The first water of the year is lucky

Before the advent of water on tap, the girl who drew the first pail of water of the year would, it was thought, be lucky in love. The first water on New Year's morning was considered to be special, and was called the 'cream' or 'flower' of the well.

The rising sun dances on Easter Sunday

In some rural communities, locals would gather to watch the sunrise on Easter Sunday. As early as the seventeenth century, superstition held that on this, the day of Christ's resurrection, the sun could be seen dancing for joy. It was even said that, if looked at through smoked glass, the image of the holy lamb could be seen in the heart of the sun.

No washing on Good Friday

To launder clothes on Good Friday was considered unlucky and sacrilegious. The water would, it was said, turn blood red, and a death might even occur as a result. Many old wives' tales forbade work of any sort being done on this day, since it was a holy day. However, it was also one of the few days of leisure that working people were allowed in the Victorian period, so often people would ignore the prohibition and tend their gardens and vegetable plots, and in fact there are an equal number of contradictory superstitions. For instance, it is said that bread baked on this day is special, and that crops planted on this day will produce a double harvest.

A future husband may be seen in the mirror at Halloween

If a single girl wishes to know the identity of her husband-to-be, she should place a veil over a mirror on Halloween. When the veil is removed, she may see the face of the man in question. Several other old wives' tales involve telling one's fortune on this day: unmarried men can see what their wife will be like by pulling up cabbage stalks and examining them. A short, fat stalk meant a similarly shaped wife!

Such stories seem to be related to the belief that the festival of Halloween is a time when supernatural spirits can be seen roaming the earth. The ghostly masks and costumes worn at this time, as well as grotesque faces carved from pumpkins, are intended to confuse and frighten away these spirits. Some theories say Halloween is a relic of the pagan festival of Samhain, which celebrates the winter solstice. Others argue that it is actually Christian in origin: Halloween is the eve of All Souls' Day, a time when the dead are remembered and their souls may be released from purgatory into heaven by the ringing of bells.

Should you hear footsteps behind you at this time of year, however, be careful not to turn round: it could be a spirit coming to take you into the afterlife!

Christmas decorations should be taken down by Twelfth Night

As is well known, it is considered unlucky to leave Christmas decorations up beyond Twelfth Night (6 January). This is a relatively recent custom, though, and prior to the twentieth century decorations were recommended to stay up until 2 February, or Candlemas. They were also put up later, and having decorations in the house before Christmas Day was not advised. Superstitions have likewise changed about their disposal. Customs from the Victorian period say that burning them is bad luck, whereas much older superstitions from the seventeenth century say just the opposite.

Father Christmas

Nowadays the idea of Santa Claus delivering presents down the chimney is synonymous with Christmas itself. The familiar rotund and jolly image of Father Christmas in his red and white suit may be a recent invention, dating from the 1930s when Coca-Cola gave him a suit that matched their logo, but the figure has an older history. According to many sources he originates in the figure of St Nicholas, a Turkish bishop of the fourth century who was well known for his benevolence to the poor. One unlikely-sounding but nevertheless charming story suggests that he was in the habit of distributing coins down the chimneys of those in need at Christmastime. On occasion, St Nicholas's charitable donations would land in stockings left by the fire to dry, thus giving rise to the tradition that Christmas presents are delivered in this unorthodox way.

Christmas cake

A traditional family Christmas would not be complete without a rich, fruity Christmas cake. The custom of making Christmas cake dates back several hundred years, and its preparation is bound up with various superstitions. In the nineteenth century it was eaten on Christmas Eve, but a piece had to be saved for Christmas Day itself. The cake mixture must be stirred by everyone in the house, and they may make a wish while doing so. However, it must be stirred in a clockwise direction, never anticlockwise – or 'widdershins' – as this brings bad luck upon the house and its inhabitants. Widdershins is said to be opposite to the direction of the sun on its course through the heavens, and so is contrary to the 'correct' or natural direction. Consequently, it is said to summon up the Devil, and many curses and spells in witchcraft involve circling in an anticlockwise motion.

Knocking on the hen house at Christmas

During the Christmas period, an unmarried girl may find out her wedding prospects by knocking on the hen coop at night. Clucking from the hens in response means she can forget about marriage for the following year, whereas a noise from the cock indicates she will soon be a bride. Another way of divining the future during the festive period involves a maid throwing a shoe over her shoulder. Should the tip point towards the door, she will not remain in service long, but, if it is the heel that faces the door, her employment is secure.

A girl may dream of her husband on St Agnes Day

St Agnes, the patron saint of virgins, was martyred on 20 January, and on this night it is reputed that an unmarried girl may ascertain who she will marry through her dreams. A variety of means were used to produce nocturnal visions of the husband-to-be. In some places she was supposed to eat a 'dumb cake', which she must bake and consume in silence directly before going to bed. In other places, she should have no food that day, and instead go to bed without breaking her fast.

The first bird seen on Valentine's Day indicates a husband-to-be

A single woman should keep a keen eye out for the first bird she sees on Valentine's morning. If the bird is a robin, it is said that her future spouse will be a sailor; if she sees a sparrow, she will marry a farmer. The lucky girl who sees a goldfinch is destined to marry a rich man, for perhaps obvious reasons.

New clothes should be worn at Easter

At least one item of new clothing should be worn at Easter to mark the end of Lent. The much-prized Easter bonnet, often the most ostentatious item in a woman's wardrobe, was part of this tradition and was one of the few occasions when ordinary people would spend their meagre wages on fancy clothes. In consequence for refusing to wear a new garment on this day, the parsimonious or slovenly will receive their punishment from the heavens in the shape of bird droppings!

Washing in the dew on May Day is good for the skin

Those worried by ageing skin should rise early on 1 May and attempt the tricky task of collecting the morning dewdrops in order to bathe in them. The magical properties of the May Day dew is said to improve the complexion and keep the skin youthful. This idea is related to other May Day superstitions that stress fecundity and rebirth. Dancing around the maypole, for instance, is a tradition rooted in pre-Christian fertility rituals: the phallic pole is decked with greenery and young maidens weave a dance around it. The same is true of the 'green man', a figure who is represented on this day by a youth clad in leaves and flowers.

A piece of Yule log prevents lightning from striking

The Yule log, a familiar image from the festive

242

period, is traditionally a block of oak or beech wood burned on Christmas Eve. Once lit, it must not be stirred on the first night, and the fire is then kept alight until Twelfth Night. A piece of the charred log is reputed to repel house fires and lightning, as well as warding off other misfortunes. Mixed with water, the burned wood could also be used as a remedy for consumption. Yule, coming from the Anglo-Saxon *geol*, originally meant the midwinter solstice, and the smouldering Yule log must have symbolised comfort and safety through the bitter depths of winter in earlier societies.

Christmas shadows indicate death

In the glow of a yuletide fire, the shadows cast on a wall are held to be significant. A close eye should be kept out for any figures that lack heads, as this means that person will not see another Christmas.

Shrove Tuesday pancakes are lucky

Lent, traditionally the period of abstinence and fasting, is immediately preceded by Shrove Tuesday or 'pancake day'. On this day, any rich food in the house such as eggs, milk and cream had to be used up and made into delicious pancakes, a custom that is still widespread today. Eating them is considered lucky as long as they are consumed before eight o'clock in the evening, after which they are not to be eaten. The reason for this injunction is mysterious, unless it was intended to aid digestion. It was not only the eating of rich foods that was permitted on Shrove Tuesday, but also other kinds of abandon. Riotous behaviour such as cock-fighting would take place, and prostitutes would be hounded out of their houses. Presumably the abstinence of Lent was considered to atone for this day of debauchery.

Jumping over fire at Easter

In the Easter period, young couples may jump over a fire to ensure they have plenty of offspring. A similar piece of folklore, common in the nineteenth century, meant that farmers would sometimes drive their cattle over a fire, or patrol the boundaries of their fields at this time of year with a flaming torch in the hope of ensuring a good yield of crops. These superstitions can be traced back to the pagan 'fire festivals' that were held to mark the end of winter and the start of spring, a time that corresponds to Eastertide in the Christian calendar. For early societies the fire rituals were important symbols of rebirth and fecundity. The idea still lingers on today in some forms: ashes and a burned lump of coal continue to be used as fertility symbols by some.

Corn dollies at harvest time

A small female figure made out of corn stalks and hung over doorways was once a common sight in farming communities, and is still sometimes seen at harvest time. The 'corn dolly' was once a central part of the harvest celebrations. As the ripe corn was cut, it was said that the 'corn mother', or spirit of the corn, was driven into the last sheaves left in the field. Accordingly, these were not harvested as usual, but made into a life-sized female effigy, clad in women's clothes and flowers, and carried back from the fields in triumph. This effigy, or smaller variations of it, was kept over winter to ensure the corn spirit allowed a sufficient harvest the next year. The practice is an old one, and at one time could be found all over Europe in one form or another.

Wassailing on Twelfth Night

On Twelfth Night, apple orchards would at one time be filled with drunken and carousing people. This practice of 'wassailing' or 'apple-howling' was intended to deter evil spirits and prevent them from interfering with the apple crop. The occasion was traditionally marked by cider drinking and the singing of special wassailing songs designed to drive away ghosts. From the earliest times and in many different religious traditions, apple orchards have been sacred places, and they were considered especially vulnerable to the attentions of malign forces. However, wassailing was also an excuse for a party to celebrate the end of the Christmas period and consume any leftover alcohol before beginning the New Year in earnest.

CHAPTER SEVENTEEN:
DAYS OF THE WEEK

'Helmut...No! Remember what day of the week it is!'

Thursday is a good day to make decisions,
but in Germany it is the unluckiest day of all.

DAYS OF THE WEEK

Sunday

As the Christian Sabbath, Sunday is traditionally a sacred day – to work during it was long held to be sacrilegious. Even activities such as sewing and knitting were frowned upon, and it was said that work done on a Sunday will come undone on a Monday. It is considered the luckiest day on which to marry, however, and children born on this day will be blessed with good fortune.

One activity that was definitely not to be undertaken on Sundays was collecting nuts. Old wives' tales from the nineteenth century state that those foolish enough to go 'nutting' on Sunday would find themselves in the company of a mysterious stranger with a cloven hoof!

Monday

Should it rain on Monday, the rest of the week will be fine, and vice versa. The origin of this old wives' tale is uncertain, but Monday is considered an unreliable and not particularly fortunate day. The birth of Cain is said to have taken place on Monday, along with Jesus's betrayal at the hands of his treacherous disciple Judas.

Another Monday superstition states that a visitor on this day means more visitors in the week to come.

Tuesday

Tuesdays are a somewhat dangerous day for women, according to folklore. They will be accident-prone and should avoid potential dangers, such as fire and sharp objects. And if possible they should schedule a medical operation for another day.

Wednesday

Those thinking of writing an important letter or asking a favour should do it on a Wednesday, since superstition says the response is likely to be more favourable.

Thursday

An important decision should be kept until Thursday, as it is more likely to be the right one if made on that day. In Germany, however, this is considered the unluckiest day of all, when any activities are doomed to failure.

Friday

Friday is said to be the day of Christ's crucifixion, Judas's hanging and Adam and Eve's expulsion from the Garden of Eden. Accordingly, it is the unluckiest day of the week, and clothes made on this day will reputedly not fit the wearer. It is not a good day to undertake a new project, move house or start a new job, and on no account should an important journey be started on a Friday. In the days of capital punishment, hangings were usually carried out on Fridays, and it is not considered an auspicious day on which to marry or to give birth, since children born on this day may be burdened with more of their share of misfortune in life.

Should an ordinary Friday fall on the thirteenth day of the month, it is especially to be feared (see page 218).

Saturday

Long or important journeys should be undertaken on a Saturday, as this is the most auspicious day of the week for travel. Those born on this day have certain psychic abilities, according to some customs, and can see spirits. It's a good idea to get your umbrella ready if a rainbow appears on a Saturday: the rest of the week will be wet.

April Fool's Day

1 April is traditionally a day for playing practical jokes on friends and family and sending them on pointless 'fool's errands'. If carried out before midday, the victim of an April Fool's hoax should take it in good spirit for fear of bad luck, but, if it is done in the afternoon, the perpetrator is the one who will be unlucky. One explanation for this strange custom is that, prior to the transition to our modern calendar in the sixteenth century, New Year celebrations took place on the first day of April. Confusion must have been common after the change, and in France it became a custom to exploit this by visiting neighbours' houses on 1 April and fooling them into thinking it was still the first

day of the year. These gullible people would then become the 'April fool'.

Other superstitions dictate that marriage on this day is inadvisable for a man, as he will be a henpecked husband. To be born on this day is generally fortunate, although those with 1 April as their birthday should be careful not to take up gambling.

Ascension Day

The weather on Ascension Day, the day Christ ascended into heaven, is said to predict that of the months ahead. Good weather on this day means a long hot summer, but bad weather means a poor harvest will be had. Eggs laid on this day are lucky, and were sometimes placed on the roof to protect the house. Rainwater that falls on Ascension Day has curative properties and may remedy bad eyes. It is a good day to give to charity, as the giver will be rewarded with riches in the long term.

Childermas

No work or ventures of any kind should be undertaken on 28 December, or 'Childermas', or they will be ill fated. Since the seventeenth century superstition has surrounded this day, which is otherwise known as Holy Innocents' Day and commemorates the day that King Herod's men put to death the firstborn children in an attempt to kill the baby Jesus. This is such an inauspicious day, in fact, that the day of the week on which it falls is considered an unlucky one for the following year.

CHAPTER EIGHTEEN:
PREDICTING THE FUTURE

'I see your father's swearing
hasn't improved...'

Ouija boards!

PREDICTING THE FUTURE

Palmistry

The practice of reading the lines and shape of a person's hand is one of the oldest and most widespread forms of divination still in use today. Some sources believe that palmistry was practised in Ancient Egypt and brought to Europe from there. Other sources point to India where sages developed a system for understanding the self and others from the lines in the hands, basing their beliefs on the Vedas, extremely ancient Hindu sacred writings. There are references to palmistry in Ancient Greek texts, and some Roman emperors apparently used palmistry to determine the character of their closest staff (Julius Caesar is said to have read his men's palms himself). Palmistry became extremely popular in Europe around the same time that the Tarot began to spread, around AD 1400. It was banned by the Catholic Church and was seen as the work of the Devil, condemning those who practised it to suspicion of witchcraft and certain death. Palmistry was popularised again after the French Revolution when interest in the occult had a renaissance, and it has seen ebbs and flows of popularity with peaks in the second half of the nineteenth century and then again in the latter half of the twentieth century.

In classical palmistry, the hand that one writes with is considered the dominant hand, whose lines are affected by events in a person's life and are constantly changing. Palmists believe that this is due to electromagnetic images from the brain being somehow imprinted in the hand. The other hand is thought to represent a person's destiny and its lines remain largely unchanged, so it is commonly the hand that is most used to predict the future, while the dominant hand is used to determine a person's life experiences and character. The most rudimentary aspects of palmistry focus on the study of the lines of the hands, the mounds, and the shape and size of hands and fingers, although everything from the shape of the fingernails to the texture of the skin is taken into account. Below are some examples, which only provide a superficial assessment of the interpretations possible with palmistry.

The main lines in the hand are the Life Line (which starts from between the thumb and index finger and goes to the wrist), the Head Line (which starts between index finger and thumb and crosses the palm) and the Heart Line (which starts below the index and middle fingers and goes down to the edge of the palm opposite the thumb). A long Heart Line is a sign of an overly romantic temperament, while a straight Heart Line is a sign of rationality. A V above the Heart Line is a sign of a warm heart. If the Life Line and the Head Line are not connected, this is a sign that the person is an independent spirit and original thinker. A double line in the Life Line is a sign of depression. A split in the Life Line suggests an important move and a shift in life plans.

259

The 'mounds' are the spaces right under fingers that look like tiny hills in the hand, or the spaces just below them. Depending on how thick and visible they are, the aspects listed below will have a greater or smaller influence on a person's life and destiny:

Jupiter (under index finger) – pride, respect, sense of religion

Saturn (under middle finger) – sadness, nostalgia, morbidity, interpersonal relationships

Sun (under ring finger) – artistic talent

Mercury (under pinkie finger) – inventiveness, creativity

Upper Mars (directly under Mercury) – courage

Moon (directly under Upper Mars) – imagination

Venus (under thumb, across from Moon) – love

Lower Mars (above Venus, across from Upper Mars) – indifference

Finally, palmistry considers the shape and size of hands and fingers. A long hand is a sign of a thoughtful and meticulous personality, a small hand is a sign of intuition and a large hand is a sign of a hesitant and cautious personality. Wide palms are a sign of a warm and affectionate character; narrow palms are a sign of selfishness. Crooked fingers are a sign of untrustworthiness, long thin fingers are a sign of an artistic temperament and pointed fingers are indicators of sensuality.

Reading tea leaves

The belief that a person's fortune may be read in a teacup is often thought to be a gypsy custom. In fact, this practice was common in Europe before the spread of tea (first brought to Europe by the Dutch in the late seventeenth century, but which only became an affordable and widely consumed beverage by the mid-nineteenth century), and can be found in many other places and societies. Before tea was imported in large quantities to Europe, fortune-tellers used herbal mixtures to look into the future. Although by the nineteenth century tea began to dominate such readings, coffee was (and still is) often used instead. The fortune-teller makes the client drink from the cup, then when just a few drops of liquid are left he or she holds the cup with the left hand and swirls the liquid counter-clockwise until the liquid is spread along the bottom of the cup. The cup is then turned upside down very gently, or alternatively the liquid is poured into a small dish. The fortune-teller looks for symbols and images inside the cup and interprets them for the client. Star signs, for example, were indicators of success, while circular traces suggested disappointment and failure.

In Roman times, fortune-tellers would look for such symbols or images in the blood and organs of animals whose insides were ritually opened with a sacred knife. Very often these animals were birds but sometimes, depending on the importance of the client, they could be larger animals such as calves or deer. It was also common to read the entrails of animals that had been killed during a hunt.

Reading tarot cards

Reading tarot cards is a form of divination of uncertain origin but which is known to have eventually spread across the Mediterranean from Italy during the late Renaissance. The origins of the images on the cards can be linked to Judeo-Christian imagery and symbolism, although some people have linked them to Indian religious cards brought by travelling gypsies, or even to symbols from Ancient Egypt. By the late eighteenth century, the Tarot had developed to the form it has today and became particularly popular in France. The Tarot of Marseilles became the most dominant form, popularised by the French occultist Antoine Court de Gébelin (1723–87) who wrote the first significant treatise on the Tarot. The greatest influence on the way tarot cards are read and interpreted today can be attributed to the work of the Hermetic Order of the Golden Dawn, an occult secret society active in London between 1888 and 1900. The author of *Dracula*, Bram Stoker, was one of its famous members, as was the poet WB Yeats. Members of this society believed that the tarot deck was part of a universal and unified esoteric system to which numerology, the Qaballah and astrology all belonged. Two of the most widely used tarot decks – the Rider Waite deck and the Throth Tarot – were designed by members of this secret society.

The deck as it is most commonly found today consists of twenty-two cards called the Major Arcana, supposedly the most magical and significant of the cards in a spread, and fifty-six Minor Arcana, resembling the playing cards in the Italian game called *tarocchi* (from which the word tarot is derived, via French). The deck follows a full sequence of numbers for four suits: Wands (also known as Batons or Rods), Cups, Swords and Coins (or Pentacles or Disks). The cards are shuffled and then distributed in a spread according to the specific needs and question of the person requesting a reading. The cards are usually arranged facing the card-reader and are given opposite and sometimes negative meaning to their normal significance if they appear upside down or 'reversed'.

Tarot cards have regained popularity in recent years and are even sometimes used in psychotherapy to facilitate discussion about difficult emotional issues.

Horoscope

The horoscope is one of the most popular systems of divination used today. The word horoscope comes from the Greek *horoscopos* which combines the word *hora* (time) and *skopos* (observer). The horoscope is based on the observation of the stars as they appear in the sky at the exact time and place of a person's birth. According to the positioning of the planets, astrologers claim to be able to read a person's destiny based on the interlocking of two circles: the circle of the twelve signs of the zodiac that reappear cyclically in the sky above the earth as they are crossed by the moon, the sun and the planets in different positions over the course of a year; and the circle of twelve houses that the circle of the Zodiac turns around every day in a twenty-four-hour cycle. The houses are divided into two parts: six above and six below the line of the horizon starting from the east. The houses that appear in the east are called the ascendant because they are on their way into the sky at the time of birth, while those beyond the zenith are called the descendant because they have already gone down. Each of the twelve houses has a unique role and meaning. The first house is the house of life; the second describes money and fortune; the third a person's relationship with other people; the fourth his or her relationship with his or her family, in particular with parents; the fifth represents children; the sixth health; the seventh represents marriage; the eighth represents death; the ninth house represents religion; the tenth represents honours and recognition; the eleventh represents friends and benefactors; and finally the twelfth house represents uncertainty and mystery.

While the full horoscope chart is unique for each individual based on their time and place of birth, there are general characteristics thought to link all people born under a specific zodiac sign, with distinctions among those born in the first, second and third ten days of the sign. Most people know their astrological sign even if they do not believe in horoscopes. Newspapers are the greatest promoters of the horoscope superstition and the practice of having horoscopes appear in daily newspapers and weekly magazines has been widespread across Europe and North America since at least the 1930s.

Bibliomancy

Bibliomancy is a very simple form of divination that was usually performed with the Bible, although any book could be used for this purpose. The person wishing to find out the answer to a particularly difficult situation or to be advised as to the best course of action would flick through the pages of the Bible and stop randomly, pointing at a spot on the page with eyes closed. Whatever the content of the paragraph on which the finger landed was considered to be the answer to the problem at hand. Ways to decipher the proper answer to the questioner's problem were, for example, to see whether the paragraph was describing a positive or negative occurrence as a way of understanding whether the outcome was to be favourable or unfavourable for the questioner. Other interpretations were dependent on the specific examples in the text and usually required a diviner to help in explaining the meaning of the passage in question. The origins of this practice are obscure but it seems reasonable to assume that, because the Bible is the sacred text *par excellence*, in the past it was seen as the word of God and a guidance in life. Even in its disembodied and randomly selected form, all answers were supposedly contained in it.

Crystallomancy

In the popular media, fortune-tellers are often depicted looking into crystal balls to see the future. This is a remnant of quite ancient forms of divination, common all over the world, where smooth reflective surfaces were consulted for images that may have given clues as to a person's future. In England the practice of scrying, the word being derived from the Old English *descry* meaning 'to reveal', was used in the Middle Ages and was normally done by looking for images in a roughly polished mirror, although it was common for the scryer to look in sword blades, ring-stones and glasses of wine. Scrying was supposedly used by a court soothsayer to uncover the Gunpowder Plot of 1605. Crystallomancy was used in Ancient Egypt by looking at a pool of ink held in a person's hand; in Polynesia the diviner would look into a hole filled with water; in South America it was usually done in a black polished stone called the *Huille-che*, although in Peru the Incas would use a large light crystal. Reflections in water were consulted almost everywhere from South Africa to Siberia.

The famous lines from the evil queen in *Snow White* – 'Mirror, mirror on the wall' – are probably connected to scrying. Today some fortune-tellers will read through crystal balls, although the practice is generally regarded with suspicion and ridicule, and is among the most discredited forms of divination.

The Ouija board

The Ouija board is a modern version of an ancient form of divination used to make contact with spirits or the ghosts of the dead. The name comes from the French and German words for 'yes' – *oui* and *ja*. The board is made up of the letters of the alphabet, numbers from 0 to 9, the words 'yes' and 'no' and a heart-shaped pointer on three felt-tipped legs. Those who wish to consult ghosts and spirits place their fingers on the heart very gently and ask a question; they then wait for the pointer to move along the Ouija board.

Precursors of the Ouija board existed in China as well as Ancient Greece where Pythagoras was among its users. Some Native Americans used *squdilatc* boards to find missing objects and people. In the mid-nineteenth century a direct ancestor of the Ouija board became very fashionable. It was called a planchette, after the name of its inventor M. Planchette. It came in the form of a heart-shaped table with three legs, one of which was a pencil. The planchette was used over paper to draw figures and letters, which would then be interpreted by a medium. The Ouija board in its contemporary form was invented in 1892 by Elija Bond and William Fuld in Baltimore, and Parker Brothers purchased rights to the production of the game in 1966. The Ouija board is second only to Monopoly in board-game sales, which shows the continued fascination people have with magic and the occult (as if *Harry Potter* sales were not enough to make this point!).

CHAPTER NINTEEN:
OLD WIVES'
TALES AND
PSEUDO-SCIENCE

'With respect, Herr Major, I believe these captured airman may be mocking us in some way.'

The belief that eating carrots makes you see in the dark can be traced back to the Second World War when British pilots were said to be eating enormous amounts of them so as to be able to see powerfully from high altitudes and in the dark.

OLD WIVES' TALES AND PSEUDO-SCIENCE

Chocolate causes acne

It is a widely held belief among teenagers, often never disputed in adulthood, that eating chocolate will cause acne breakouts. There is little scientific evidence that acne is affected by diet at all, although some dermatologists argue that in rare cases it may be connected to some food allergies. The greatest factors affecting acne are genetics, hormones (during periods or during puberty), washing the face too often, using oily cosmetics or side effects of certain medications. Though stress does not directly cause acne, it can aggravate existing outbreaks.

Masturbating will make your hands hairy, m
you mentally ill or infertile – you might eve
go blind!

The argument that masturbation was a hi
dangerous activity was clearly devised
discourage its practice. Girls were often told
masturbating could make them sterile, but tl
is no medical evidence to suggest this is the c
There is little in medical texts concerr
masturbation prior to the mid-eightee
century, although in many religious societi
Europe and in North America all pleasures of
flesh were frowned upon, especially if perfor
outside of wedlock. Despite this, there is
direct mention of masturbation in the B
although a famous passage in Genesis 38:9 re
'And Onan knew that the seed should not be
and it came to pass, when he went in unto
brother's wife, that he spilled it on the grou
lest that he should give seed to his brother.
the thing which he did displeased the L
wherefore he slew him also.' This was o
interpreted as a sign that masturbation was a
and it also accounts for the use of the
'onanism' to refer to masturbation. In fact, r

274

theologians today suggest that what displeased the Lord was Onan's exploitative treatment of his brother's wife.

Ancient beliefs in the 'homunculus', or little man, saw the act of masturbation by men as a waste of potential life, since it was thought that in sperm was a tiny and fully formed little man who would simply be nourished by the female body. By the nineteenth century, an entire field of 'masturbation science' emerged, suggesting that any form of masturbation had terrible physical consequences on the bodies of men and women, and even suggesting that having intercourse more than twelve times a year was dangerous for a man's health. Anti-masturbation devices were invented and very successfully marketed, and school texts warned against the dangers of masturbation with horrific pictures. Today doctors argue that masturbation is a natural form of release and has no dangerous consequences to the body except for the psychological damages of stress and guilt associated with it when people feel it is a sin.

If you go outside without a coat or with wet hair, you will catch a cold or even get pneumonia

It is commonly believed that to stay out in the cold will cause a person to catch a cold, or maybe even pneumonia. A cold, however, is caused by a virus, while pneumonia is caused by bacteria such as the *Streptococcus pneumoniae* and neither is related to temperature or bad weather. Many people still believe that getting cold can damage the overall working of the immune system, perhaps incorrectly assuming that getting a fever is one of our body's remedies against infection. There is no scientific evidence, however, for any connection between lowered body temperature and the immune system's ability to function effectively.

Hair myths

It is commonly believed that to shave one's head or to cut it short will make it grow thicker than before. This is not true. What does occur is that it looks more coarse because the middle of the hair is exposed at the end and the hair loses flexibility when very short, which makes it feel rougher, but this is down to its mobility, not its actual thickness. There are many other common misconceptions about hair loss and growth not corroborated by science: it is thought that cutting hair when the moon is waxing will make it grow back faster than if it is cut when the moon is on the wane, when it will also lose its shine. This superstition can probably be connected to observations of the tide, or to the even more simplistic sense that when the moon is waxing it is growing while when it is waning it is getting smaller. It is also thought that pulling a grey hair will cause two more to grow in its place, which is also untrue and may have been meant to punish the vanity of people who were concerned about seeming old. Finally, a very widespread belief is that hair loss is inherited from the mother's side of the family. The origins of this misconception can be ascribed to early genetics studies, which initially seemed to have found a correlation between the likelihood that a man would go bald if his mother's brothers were also bald. In fact, hair loss can be inherited from either side of the family and sometimes skips generations.

Carrots make you see in the dark

Although carrots contain vitamin A, a vitamin useful for maintaining healthy vision, they do not contain enough actually to improve eyesight. The origins of this myth can be traced back to the Second World War when British pilots were said to be eating enormous amounts of carrots so as to be able to see powerfully from high altitudes and in the dark. This rumour was actively spread as a way to dissemble the fact that the radar had been invented and was being used against the enemy. It is true that vitamin A deficiency can cause night blindness, but this does not mean that eating large quantities of carrots will give people particularly strong eyesight.

CHAPTER TWENTY:
FLOWERS AND TREES

'Damn...I'm sorry Carruthers old chap, but it
looks as if we're going to have to kiss.'

It's unlucky not to kiss under the mistletoe!

FLOWERS AND TREES

Lilies

Lilies are mentioned in the Bible. They were thought to have sprung from Eve's tears when she and Adam were banished from the Garden of Eden. They were also said to have grown in the Garden of Gethsemane from drops of sweat fallen from the body of Christ the night before the crucifixion. Their growth out of Christ's sweat is clearly a symbol of the Resurrection, which is why lilies are often used in churches at Easter. Traditionally lilies are also associated with the Virgin Mary and with motherhood. In most pictorial depictions of the Annunciation, the moment when the archangel Gabriel appears in front of Mary to tell her that she is expecting the son of God, lilies appear, either carried by the angel or growing close to the Virgin Mary as symbols of her purity and chastity. At the time of Mary's death, when her body was said to have ascended to heaven, St Thomas found lilies in place of Mary's body in her coffin.

Due to their association with the body of the Virgin Mary and with the Resurrection, lilies were thought to be particularly powerful flowers for warding off evil spirits and fighting witchcraft. Lilies of the valley were considered unlucky, especially when brought indoors, since they were thought to represent the tears of the Virgin.

Elder
Since at least the fifth century, the elder plant was often associated with death and it was thought that to smell it – and especially to sleep under it – could cause death or disease. Dead bodies were sometimes buried with it as a precaution against evil spirits, and because of this association it was considered unlucky to make cribs out of elder wood. During the Stone Age, arrows were carved into the shape of elder leaves and it is possible

that an association between death and the elder plant existed even then. It was thought that to burn the elder plant would bring the Devil into the house, and that witches would sometimes disguise themselves as elder plants if they were being chased, especially at night. In Denmark it was believed that to sit under the elder tree on Midsummer Night would allow a person to see the king of the fairies riding by. In Serbia, branches of elder plant were traditionally used during weddings to bring the couple good luck. There are several superstitions about the dangers of breaking elder trees, and in England it was common practice to ask the tree for permission before pruning it so as to avoid misfortune.

Roses

Roses have traditionally been assigned several superstitious meanings. If they were seen to grow out of season, it was thought to be an omen of bad luck for a year. To be carrying, and especially wearing, a rose and to see it shed its petals was an omen of death, as was dreaming of roses. The German word *Rosengarten* means rose garden, but is sometimes used to refer to a cemetery, probably because roses represented death, and roses were often the preferred flowers in cemeteries in Germany and Austria. Even today, if a person was thought to be particularly benevolent, philanthropic and generous during their life, it is common to place a bouquet of red roses on their grave; and roses are also the flower of choice for the graves of lovers. Roses, like lilies, are associated with the Virgin Mary, and thus the rosary – a series of repeated prayers addressed to the Virgin – derives its name from the idea that the verses are offered to her like bunches of roses.

Roses have also been associated with silence since antiquity. A myth concerning Eros, the god of love, recounts that he gave Harpocrates, the god of silence, a rose to cloak the weaknesses of the gods in silence so that humans would not know of them, and the Latin expression *sub rosa* – 'in secret' – derived from this. It is based on this myth that the ceilings of council halls and confessionals were traditionally decorated with roses: everything said under the rose was to be confidential.

Mistletoe

Mistletoe is best known for its role in allowing stolen kisses to take place under it during Christmas. Although it does seem that mistletoe was worshipped in Europe in ancient times and is said to have been used in medicine, the practice of kissing under it is a modern invention, dating back only as far as the nineteenth century. There are records of mistletoe being used as a protection against witchcraft in the seventeenth century, and it may have become a common Christmas decoration precisely to protect the household from witches during the dangerous transitional time of Christmas. The kissing superstition probably originated in a Victorian game in which a young man was allowed to give a woman only as many kisses under the mistletoe as there were berries on the bushel. The berries the young man would then present the woman with were thought to bring her good luck, fertility and prosperity for the coming year. Another superstition probably stemmed from this game, suggesting that not kissing under the mistletoe would mean not marrying that year, something rather logical since if a woman did not have a sweetheart to kiss at

Christmas it was unlikely that she would be getting married that year, especially given the long engagement practices common in Victorian times. Today the superstition suggests simply that it is lucky to kiss under the mistletoe and that two people finding themselves below it must kiss to avoid misfortune stemming from breaking the Christmas rules.

Four-leaf clover

The four-leaf clover is probably the most famous of all good-luck symbols, depicted over and over on lottery tickets, greeting cards and lucky-charm amulets and jewels. Superstition has it that it is particularly lucky to find a four-leaf clover when walking through a field, and each leaf on the clover is meant to represent one of the four different spheres in which the clover is thought to have a beneficial effect: wealth, fame, love and health. This superstition has been documented to have existed as far back as the seventeenth century, but may be even older, and it clearly stems from the relative rarity of finding such a clover in a field of ordinarily three-leafed clovers. In the past, the four-leaf clover was thought to provide protection against witches and to allow those who wore it to see through and expose any tricks played by witches and fairies. In Britain, to find a four-leaf clover was thought to be a sign that one was about to encounter one's soulmate, and in some accounts a four-leaf clover worn on the jacket was thought to provide young men with protection against military draft. Today the four-leaf clover is simply considered lucky in a more general way.

Daisies

According to superstition, plucking a daisy's petals and counting them off to the rhyme 'He loves me, he loves me not' until the last petal is meant to provide an answer about a person's object of desire or about the faithfulness of a sweetheart. This superstition is relatively recent, probably stemming from late Victorian children's games, sometimes combined with the rhyme 'Rich man, poor man, farmer, ploughman, thief' – meant to determine the profession of a little girl's future husband. In the past it was thought that to put a daisy root under one's pillow would produce dreams about one's future partner. It was also common practice to eat the first daisy one saw in the spring in order to have good luck for the rest of the year. In some accounts, daisies were thought to be given to the earth by the spirits of stillborn babies in order to provide their parents with some consolation for their untimely deaths.

Myrtle

Because in ancient times myrtle was associated with the goddess Venus, it is a symbol of love and fertility. In Roman times brides would carry bouquets of myrtle at their wedding and Queen Victoria apparently had myrtle in her bridal bouquet. It is considered particularly lucky for a newlywed couple to plant bushes of myrtle on each side of their front door to ensure that love and peace do not leave their household. In the past, the happiness of a marriage was apparently gauged by the health of the myrtle plant outside the front door. It was considered unlucky to destroy such plants, as that would be equivalent to destroying the peace and happiness of a marriage. It was also considered an omen of death if such plants withered and died of their own accord, and myrtle was sometimes planted on the gravestones of loved ones by grieving widows or widowers.

Dandelions

Children love blowing away the seeds of dandelions once they have turned into 'clocks' or, as the writer Vladimir Nabokov once wrote, 'turned from suns to moons'. In a British superstition dating back to the nineteenth century, it was thought that people could predict the number of years separating them from their wedding day based on the number of breaths they would have to take in order to blow off all the seeds of the dandelion. Another version of the superstition saw the number of breaths as denoting the number of children one would have. Dandelions were traditionally used in herbal infusions aimed at curing urinary tract infections. This may explain why it was once thought that picking a dandelion would cause one to wet the bed.

CHAPTER TWENTY-ONE:
INTERNATIONAL TALISMANS

The evil eye!

INTERNATIONAL TALISMANS

 Middle Eastern talismans protecting against the evil eye
Belief in the evil eye is extremely ancient and it is spread across the Middle East and the Mediterranean basin. A common talisman used to protect against the evil eye is a silver or iron charm containing a glass eye, usually blue. Sometimes the eye will be contained inside an equilateral triangle, representing the power of the Trinity and of the perfect number three. Other such talismans also contain a silver horseshoe, or are simply formed in the shape of a large blue and white glass eye.

Native American Hopi and Zuni Fetishes

 In Native American Hopi and Zuni societies, it is common for people to carry around carved fetishes, which are thought to provide them with protection and guidance in certain areas of life. The fetishes are kept in small pouches and worn around the neck and are sometimes given offerings of food. The most common fetishes and their meanings are as follows:

Bear

Power, strength, ability to evaluate current environment, introspection, spiritual journey through life

Buffalo

Endurance, ability to rise above weakness, great emotional courage

Butterfly

The art of transformation, the ability to know or change the mind

Coyote

Humour, master trickster who tricks himself, laughter, foolishness

Duck

Spirits of those who have passed on

Eagle

Creator, teacher, loyalty, great integrity, connection to Heaven

Frog

Bringer of rain, abundance and fertility

Hawk

Messenger of the gods, ability to observe the obvious in everything you do

Horned lizard

Conservation of natural resources, self-reliance, longevity

Horse

Healing, swiftness, strength, enlightenment

Mountain lion
Leadership, resourcefulness, the power to lead without insisting that others follow

Owl
Ability to see what others cannot, essence of true wisdom, deception

Rabbit
Virtue, serenity, low curiosity, quiet talent, restrained passion, the special guardian of women in childbirth, long life

Snake
Life, death, rebirth, power of creation, power of transmutation

Turtle
The oldest symbol of Mother Earth, longevity

Wolf
Teacher, pathfinder, sharing of your knowledge, a never-ending journey

Italian amulet against _malocchio_

In Italy and in other parts of southern Europe, people still carry around amulets made of coral (or in their cheaper form in red plastic) depicting the hands in the shape of the Devil's horns, as protection against the evil eye and misfortune in general. The amulet derives from the gesture used to counter the presence of the evil eye or a mention of the Devil or any other evil force, where the second and third finger of the hand are folded leaving the index and pinkie pointing downwards, in the shape of the Devil's horns. It is also common to see amulets in the shape of a red coral horn, sometimes topped by a gold crown depicting the horn of the Devil contained by the crown of the Virgin Mary. To point the Devil's horns at ill-wishers or the Devil himself is to deflect their evil intentions and direct them back at those wishing one harm.

**Japanese Maneki Neko,
the lucky beckoning cat**

In Japan it is customary to keep a Maneki Neko or

beckoning cat in one's house, or on the counter or in the window of a shop. The fat cat figurine, depicted wearing a bell and holding a coin on one paw with the other paw up in the air, is thought to bring happiness to the home, and customers and prosperity to a shop. While it may look to westerners like the cat is waving, it is in fact making the gesture of beckoning the Japanese way. In Japan, in fact, people beckon by holding their hands up with the palm facing forward and then open and close their fingers over the palm. When the Maneki Neko is shown holding up a left paw, it is supposed to bring customers; when it is shown holding up the right paw, it is supposed to indicate money. The different colours of the Maneki Neko have different meanings: red gives protection against evil spirits and illness; gold brings wealth; white indicates purity; and black protects against evil. The black Maneki Neko is favoured by women as it is thought to give special protection against sexual harassment.

Although there seems to be mention of the Maneki Neko as early as the seventeenth century, it became popular in its present form in the mid-nineteenth century, when it also started to be used as a piggy bank. There are various theories about why the Maneki Neko became popular around that time, one of which suggests that it was because the Meiji government had banned sexually explicit sculptures from being displayed in the windows of brothels, so the cat initially represented a beckoning prostitute. It may have been considered funny and later marketed as an object aimed at attracting other kinds of customers.

The Khamsa (Fatima's Hand), or the Hamesh (Miriam's Hand)

Present in both Jewish and Islamic iconography, the Khamsa or the Hamesh is an ancient symbol probably predating both religions. Although the Koran forbids the use of talismans, the Khamsa is widely produced and used as decoration especially in Egypt. It refers to the hand of Fatima, the beloved daughter of Muhammad, and it is thought that the five

299

fingers of the hand represent the five pillars of Islam, which are core features of the Sunni Faith. The Jewish 'Hamesh', or 'Chamesh', is thought to represent the hand of Miriam, the sister of Moses and Aaron. In both the Islamic and the Jewish tradition the hand symbol is thought to provide protection against the evil eye and to represent the hand of God, acting benevolently in people's lives.

CHAPTER TWENTY-TWO:
AROUND
THE WORLD

It is unlucky to praise a baby in China. It is customary to talk badly of other people's children so that parents can convert what is said into compliments…

AROUND THE WORLD

Praising a baby in China

It is considered very unlucky to praise a baby in China because it is thought that to do so attracts the attention of ghosts and demons. It is therefore customary to talk badly about the child and suggest it has no good qualities. Parents are to convert all bad things said about their baby into compliments in their heads.

Meeting a nun on the street in Italy

In Italy it is believed to be unlucky to see a nun on the street, and necessary to take precautionary measures should you do so. The best way to avoid what is called *sfiga di suora* – a nun's bad luck – is for a man to touch his testicles and for a woman to touch wood or metal. Another common practice, usually adopted by children, is to 'pass on' the bad fortune by touching somebody else and saying *'Sfiga di suora'*. The origins of this superstition can be linked to the fact that until the mid-twentieth century it was mostly nuns that worked as nurses in hospitals. To see a nun in one's neighbourhood meant that somebody was seriously ill, so it was considered bad luck, possibly announcing death or illness in the family.

Meeting a man whose beard, moustache and hair are different colours in the US

In the United States of America it is thought that men who have their hair, beard and moustache of two different colours are not to be trusted. There is a rhyme to remind people of this mistrust:

Beware of that man
Be he friend or brother
Whose hair is one colour
And moustache is another.

Americans also believe, as do many in the British Isles and other European countries, that men with red beards are suspicious.

Dreaming of being snatched by a snake in Thailand

In Thailand it is thought that if a person dreams of being held tightly by a snake this is an omen that they will soon meet their soulmate. The size and colour of the snake can sometimes be seen as an indication of the type of person they will fall for: dreaming of a small brown snake, for example, may be a sign that the person's soulmate will be a rather short person of dark complexion.

Chewing gum at night in Turkey

It is considered very unlucky to chew gum at night-time in Turkey. People say that those who do so are chewing the flesh of a dead body.

Starting a business on a Tuesday in Greece

Tuesday is considered the most unlucky day in Greece and it is therefore considered extremely unlucky to start a business or any new venture on that day of the week. This superstition is thought to date back to Tuesday, 29 May 1453, which was the day the Greek city of Constantinople (Istanbul today) fell to the Ottoman Turks.

Listening to good wishes and praise in Russia

If a person is praised, given good wishes, or if one's good fortune is mentioned, in Russia, it is very important for that person to spit three times over his or her left shoulder while knocking on wood at the same time. This is customary in order to avoid losing the good qualities or good fortune being spoken of.

Jumping over a child in Turkey

Parents in Turkey are advised not to jump over a child in getting from one part of a room to another because this is thought to cause the child to remain as short as he or she is at the time of the jump.